CERTIFICATE IN
COUNSELLING STUDIES

Alice Miller

BANISHED

KNOWLEDGE

Facing Childhood Injuries

Translated from the German
by Leila Vennewitz

Published by VIRAGO PRESS Limited 1990
20–23 Mandela Street, Camden Town, London NW1 0HQ

TRANSLATOR'S NOTE

The following passage occurs in the Preface to the 2nd edition of Ashley Montagu's *Touching: The Human Significance of the Skin* (New York: Harper & Row, 1986):

One regret that every writer must have is that there does not exist in English a word which specifically refers to both sexes. In this edition I first attempted to remedy that situation by employing "it" as a substitute for the customary masculine pronouns. The result was an unacceptable impersonality which, combined with the awkward repetitiveness of "he or she" and "his or hers," rendered the change repellent. I, therefore, have adhered to customary usage. It is, of course, to be understood that in all instances both sexes are implied. This book is about human beings, not objects, and no baby is an "it" to its mother, nor should it be to anyone else.

I wish to express my great appreciation to the author, Dr. Alice Miller, for the close cooperation I have enjoyed with her. I also wish to thank my husband, William, who has accompanied me throughout the work of this translation with his never-failing, expert assistance.

CONTENTS

CONTENTS

CONTENTS

PREFACE

UNLIKE ANIMALS, which generally become self-reliant shortly after birth, the human infant remains dependent on others for a very long time. He comes into the world as a bundle of needs, relying totally on the warmth of human arms, watchful eyes, and tender caresses. Incubators and electric heat are merely a very inadequate substitute for human contact, and the touch of cold instruments can be torture. A baby requires the certainty that he will be protected in every situation, that his arrival is desired, that his cries are heard, that the movements of his eyes are responded to and his fears calmed. The baby needs assurance that his hunger and thirst will be satis-

1

fied, his body lovingly cared for, and his distress never ignored.

Is that asking too much? Under some circumstances it is much too much, a great burden, while under others it is a joy and an enrichment. It all depends on what the parents themselves experienced in the past and what they have to give. Nevertheless, every child depends on others for the satisfaction of his needs because he cannot look after himself. Although he can scream for help, he relies entirely on those around him to hear his cries, take them seriously, and satisfy the underlying needs rather than, in an excess of hatred, punishing the screams or even preventing them by means of tranquilizers.

The only possible recourse a baby has when his screams are ignored is to repress his distress, which is tantamount to mutilating his soul, for the result is an interference with his ability to feel, to be aware, and to remember.

When this innate ability to feel cannot blossom, a person cannot know later in life what it means, for example, to be defenseless and so is incapable of providing his or her own child with the protection and love in which this child will likewise stand in urgent need. Parents who have never known love, who on coming into the world met with coldness, insensitivity, indifference, and blindness and whose entire childhood and youth were spent in this atmosphere, are unable to bestow love—indeed, how can they, since they have no idea of what love is and can be? Nevertheless, their children will survive. And, like their parents, they too will not remember the torments to which they were once exposed, because those torments, together with the needs related to them, have all been repressed: that is, completely banished from consciousness.

A human being born into a cold, indifferent world will regard his situation as the only possible one. Everything that person later comes to believe, advocate, and deem right is founded on his first formative experiences. Today we have conclusive evidence that this cost of survival not only is much too high for the individual but also turns out to be the greatest threat to all humanity. In the fifties, experiments showed that monkeys separated from their mothers and raised with fabric dummy mothers had no motherly instincts when they later gave birth. And we have statistics showing clear connections between early neglect and abuse and subsequent adult violence. Why is it that hardly any conclusions are being drawn from these statistics? The repression of past torments and its cost render people deaf to the screams of children and blind to the obvious connections. Thus the factors so clearly revealed by the statistics are ignored to block the eruption of once repressed pain, to prevent the recognition of the truth.

In the heart of snowbound Paris, in the cold January of 1987, a vagrant came upon a plastic bag containing a crying newborn infant. The parents, not wanting to keep him, had left him to his fate. The Arab clochard who, unlike other passers-by, was not in a hurry to reach a warm home (because he had none) saved the infant's life. If he had not listened to the baby's crying and if the baby had not been able to signal his plight, the child would have frozen to death. That baby survived freezing temperatures, and other babies have survived just as drastic physical circumstances: A baby found crying in the ruins of the Mexico City earthquake of 1985, for instance, had lived several days without food.

This great adaptability of the newborn infant to our cruel world, this toughness, has since time immemorial misled people to believe that one can inflict anything on a child with impunity: completely neglect him, hold lighted cigarettes against his skin, shake him, throw him against the wall, yell at him. Until recently no one corrected these notions because in their defenselessness injured children could not speak about the torments they were exposed to; their signals went unnoticed. And later, as adults, they had themselves forgotten such experiences, or at least the memory was not vivid enough to cause them to speak of them. But somehow they must have known, their brains had obviously stored the knowledge, for in a sort of compulsive repetition they passed on their traumatic experiences to their children, again oblivious to the consequences.

To demonstrate the hidden sources of violence, I described Adolf Hitler's childhood in my book *For Your Own Good*. My aim was to show how the life of a mass murderer reflects the countless murders to which the child was subjected. I described the phenomenon for the same reasons others might describe a virus: to prevent the further spread of the disease or the phenomenon as the result of ignorance. This description was necessary because many people still have no idea that they are placing dynamite in our world when they abuse their children physically or even "only" psychically. They describe their actions as proper and necessary. Others are of the opinion that such behavior, although not quite proper, is unavoidable since children are sometimes difficult and their parents overtaxed: They "can't help themselves"

4

and lash out. To my mind, both views are mistaken, inhumane, and dangerous.

It is quite simply not true that human beings must continue compulsively to injure their children, to damage them for life and thus destroy our future. When I wrote *The Drama of the Gifted Child,* while under the influence of psychoanalytic thinking, I still believed that such a cycle of abuse was inevitable. Now I know that that is not true. Infectious diseases need not spread if the virus is known. Injuries can heal and need not be passed on, provided they are not ignored. It is perfectly possible to awaken from sleep and, in that waking state, to be open to the messages from our children that can help us never again to destroy life but rather to protect it and allow it to blossom.

Not to take one's own suffering seriously, to make light of it or even to laugh at it, is considered good manners in our culture. This attitude is even called a virtue, and many people (at one time including myself) are proud of their lack of sensitivity toward their own fate and above all toward their own childhood. I have tried to show in my books why the fatal belief that such an attitude is desirable can so stubbornly persist, as well as the tragic conditions it helps to conceal. People from various countries constantly tell me, with great relief, that after reading *The Drama of the Gifted Child* they felt for the first time in their lives something like empathy for the abused or even battered child they had once been. They say that they have more respect for themselves than formerly and that they have become more precisely aware of their needs and feelings. "You have described my life in that book—how did you know about it?" is something I often hear.

How did I know about it? Today I no longer find it difficult to answer this question. Today I know: It wasn't the books, or my teachers, or my philosophical studies, or my training as a psychoanalyst that provided me with this knowledge. On the contrary. Their mystifying conceptualizations, their turning aside from reality, prevented me far too long from recognizing the truth. Surprisingly, it was only the abused, exploited, fossilized child in me, condemned so long ago to speechlessness, that finally found her feelings and thus her speech and painfully told me her story. It was *this* story that I began to describe in *The Drama of the Gifted Child,* and many, many people recognized their own story in it as if I were holding up a mirror to them.

In my fourth book, *Pictures of a Childhood,* I described in more detail how my encounter with this child came about after she surfaced from her banishment and how I could offer her the protection she needed to feel her pain and be able to talk about it.

The discovery that I had been an abused child, that from the very beginning of my life I had had to adapt to the needs and feelings of my mother, with no chance whatever to feel any of my own, came as a great surprise to me. The discovery of my total helplessness at that time also showed me not only the power of repression that all my life had kept me away from the truth but as well the impotence of psychoanalysis, whose misleading theories further reinforced this repression. For although I had undergone two complete analyses as part of my training, the analysts had been unable to shake my version of the happy childhood I was supposed to have had. It was only my spontaneous painting, which I took up in 1973, that gave me the first unadulterated access to my early reality.

In my paintings I came face to face with the terrorism exerted by my mother, at the mercy of which I had lived for so many years. For no one in my environment, not even my kind father, could ever notice or question the child abuse committed under the cloak of childrearing. If but a single person had understood at that time what was going on and had come to my defense, my entire life would have taken a different course. That person could have helped me to recognize the cruelty and not tolerate it for decades as something normal and necessary, at the expense of my own life.

This absence of enlightened witnesses in my life may have contributed to my desire, through my books, to inform potential helpers about the suffering child. By "potential helpers" I mean all those who do not shrink from unequivocally taking the side of the child and protecting him from power abuse on the part of adults. In our child-inimical society such people are still rare, but their number is growing.

My spontaneous painting helped me not only to discover my personal history but also to liberate myself from the mental compulsions and concepts of my upbringing and training, which I recognized as being wrong, misleading, and fatal. The more I learned to follow my impulses in the free play of color and form, the weaker became my ties to aesthetic and other conventions. I was not out to paint beautiful pictures; even painting good pictures was not important to me. I wanted only to help the truth burst forth. I eventually succeeded, in 1983, with the aid of Konrad Stettbacher's therapy method, with which I deal in more detail later in this book. But even before that, I was beginning to see, with greater clarity, how the constructs of psychoanalysis block access to the truth. That is what I have tried to describe in my books to open the eyes of the victims of this blockage and at least save them the laborious path of my own search. This has earned me much hatred but also much gratitude.

By the time of my therapy I had grasped the fact that I had been abused as a child because my parents had undergone similar experiences in their childhoods and had learned to regard that abuse as having been for their own good. Because they—like the analysts in my training— were not allowed to feel and thus understand what had happened to them in the past, they were unable to recognize the abuse and passed it on to me without a trace of guilty feelings.

I realized there was absolutely nothing I could do to change the history of my parents and teachers that had so blinded them. But I felt that, in spite of all this, I can and must try to demonstrate to young parents, and above all to future parents, the dangers of the misuse of their power, to sensitize them and sharpen their ears to their child's signals.

I can do this if I help the child—hitherto a victim condemned to silence, deprived of rights—to speak out, if I describe his suffering from his perspective and not from that of the adult. For it is from this very child that I received vital messages, answers to questions that had remained unanswered throughout my entire study of philosophy and psychoanalysis yet had refused to cease preoccupying me all my life. Only when the actual reasons for my childhood fears and pains became clear to me in their full extent did I understand what grown men and women must keep at a distance throughout their lives and why, instead of facing up to the truth, they prefer, for instance, to organize a gigantic, atomic self-destruction without the slightest inkling of its absurdity. For me, the absurdity acquired its compelling logic once I was able, thanks to the therapy, to locate the missing piece, the hitherto strictly guarded secret of childhood. For when we no longer need to confront the child's suffering blindly, we suddenly realize that it is up to us adults, depending on how we treat our newborn infants, either to turn them into future monsters or to allow them to grow up into feeling, and hence responsible, human beings.

In this book my aim is to share with others the knowledge I have gained over the last few years. The extent of my success remains to be seen. However, since I am convinced that this knowledge of the child's situation can lead people to a radical and urgently necessary rethinking, I wish to leave nothing untried.

I

HUMANITY'S
FATEFUL SLEEP

ONE

A SAINT NICHOLAS
CELEBRATION

THERE ARE MANY EXAMPLES of how the repression
of our suffering destroys our empathy for the suffering of
others. Let me pick out an ostensibly harmless illustration and examine it in detail.

One day early in December, while walking through the
forest, I encountered a celebration. A number of families
had come with their children, lighted candles at the edge
of the forest, and invited Saint Nicholas. Traditionally,
this celebration is preceded by the young mothers informing Saint Nicholas of the attitudes and behavior of
their children and the saint registering the sins in a big
book so that he can speak to the children as if he were all-

13

knowing. The mothers hope thereby to gain support for their childrearing methods, and that is what they get. All year long they can allude to his words: "Saint Nicholas sees everything, you've heard it yourself—make sure that next time he's satisfied with you!"

How did it proceed, this celebration whose chance witness I was? About ten children, one after the other, were first chided and then praised by Saint Nicholas. Only one little girl was not rebuked, presumably because her mother had not felt the need to inform a strange man, in writing, of her child's transgressions. Saint Nicholas spoke approximately as follows: "Where is little Vera?" A small girl, scarcely two years old, with a trusting, expectant look, came forward and gazed up with candid curiosity into the saint's face. "I must say, Vera, Saint Nicholas is not at all pleased that you don't always like to put away your toys by yourself. Mommy is too busy. You're old enough to understand that when you've finished playing you must put away your toys and also that you should share them like a good girl with your little brother and not keep everything for yourself. Let's hope next year will see an improvement. Saint Nicholas will be looking into your room to see whether you've improved. But he has also found out some good things: You help your mother to clear the table after meals, and you can play nicely by yourself and sometimes draw pictures too, without Mommy having to sit beside you. I like that very much, for Mommy is too busy to sit with you all the time; don't forget she also has your little brother and your daddy to care for, and she needs a Vera who can do things on her own. Well now, Vera, have you also learned a little song for Saint Nicholas?" Vera stood there too scared to utter a sound, so instead her mother sang the song Vera had prepared. At the end the child was given a small package from Saint Nicholas's sack.

Now it was the next child's turn: "Well, well, Stefan, you're still using a pacifier; you're much too big for that, you know [Stefan was scarcely two and a half]. If you brought along your pacifier you might as well give it to Saint Nicholas right away [the other children laughed]. No, you haven't got it with you? Then tonight you will put it on your bedside table or give it to your little brother. You don't need a pacifier anymore, you're much too big for that. Saint Nicholas has also noticed that you're not always a good little boy at the table, always interrupting when the grown-ups are talking; but you must let the grown-ups talk, you're still much too small to be constantly interrupting the others."

Little Stefan seemed on the verge of tears; he stood there looking thoroughly scared, shamed in front of all the others, and I tried to make him feel that he wasn't completely without rights. I said to Saint Nicholas: "A minute ago you were telling him he's too big for a pacifier, and now you say he's too small to speak up at table. Stefan himself will know very well when he no longer needs his pacifier." At that point I was interrupted by some of the mothers because my words were highly inappropriate to this sacred ceremony, and one mother put me in my place: "Here it's up to Saint Nicholas to say what Stefan must do!"

So I abandoned my good intentions and restricted myself to taping the scene on a small recorder because I could hardly believe my ears. The celebration continued exactly as it had begun. No one noticed the cruelty, no one saw the stricken faces (although the fathers were constantly taking flash pictures). No one noticed that

15

each of the reprimanded children ended up not being able to remember the words of the little poem or song; that they couldn't even find their voices, could hardly say thank you; that none of the children smiled spontaneously, that they all looked petrified with fear. No one noticed that what was actually being enacted was a vicious power play at the expense of the children.

Thus, for instance, a little boy of scarcely three had to listen to the following: "Well, well, Kaspar, I see that you throw your toys around. That's very dangerous; you might hit your mother on the head, and then she'll have to go to bed and won't be able to look after you anymore, she won't be able to cook, and then you won't get anything to eat. Or you might hit your brother or your daddy and then they'll both have to go to bed, Mommy will be busy with them and have to bring them their meals. Then you won't be able to play anymore, you'll have to help Mommy." And on and on in this vein.

I was by no means sure whether this little boy had understood anything at all, he looked so utterly confused. But if he was able to absorb any of it, it was the dissatisfied tone and the message that he could wreak havoc on his family and as a punishment would have to be deprived of his mother. Whether he really understood what made him such a threat to his family is very doubtful, but his apprehension was abundantly evident. His smiling mother, however, seemed quite unaware of this.

Each of the children wanted to please Saint Nicholas, wanted to hear something nice; but before the children could hear those nice things, they had to listen to the bad things they had done. That was enough to interfere with their openness and attention. The reprimand engendered fear, and they had to repress this fear to retain pleasant memories of the occasion—which was exactly what the parents expected of them. Although the unconscious can never rid itself of the certainty that even the small child is wicked, the child's consciousness will cling for decades to the beautiful version of that celebration. It follows that the future parents will treat their children in exactly the same way, likewise expecting from them great delight in the lovely ceremony without wondering why the children have to be exposed to such a procedure in the first place.

The greatest virtue attested to by Saint Nicholas in his capacity of the parents' mouthpiece was the children's ability to play by themselves and not need their mothers. In one case he actually said, word for word: "I have something good about you to report: You help your mommy clear the table, and that's very necessary because Mommy can't do everything alone. But don't forget to put away your toys nicely, Mommy can't help you with that, you have to do that by yourself." This reasoning appeared quite logical to Nicholas: The three-year-old doesn't have to be helped by Mommy, the child must help Mommy. In the same way, helpfulness was one of the children's positive contributions: You don't mind being alone, you can put away your toys nicely, you can share with your little brother, and you can manage without your mother. Cause for rebuke, on the other hand, was talking, standing up for oneself, not being grown up yet, and the natural needs of the child for help, affection, and consolation. To the three-year-old boy who has a baby brother and is obliged to look on while his mother nurses the baby, the pacifier is often nothing but a consolation in his loneliness, a help in his effort to suppress the feelings of jealousy that he wishes to spare his mother.

At first sight it was amazing that no adult at the Saint Nicholas celebration noticed the children's fear or the threat represented by the saint. The mothers didn't seem in any way unloving; they made an effort to help the children, to sing their songs or recite their poems. They were obviously concerned with providing their children with a lovely ceremony, an experience on which the children were supposed to look back with joy, emotion, and gratitude. Perhaps they did achieve their aim if all the children managed to retain only the pleasant memory in their consciousness. But without a doubt the children must also have had to repress intense feelings: fear of this strange man who seemed to know all their misdeeds like an all-knowing God, impotent rage at having nowhere to hide as a child, and shame over the public rebuke. What seemed worse to me, however, was that the children were left to cope alone with all these feelings; it was quite obvious that the smiling mothers had no understanding of their children's mixed emotions, or they would never have exposed them to such a situation.

Why did these mothers lack understanding? Why did they all, with one exception, put their children at the mercy of a stranger, delegate their authority to him, denounce their children, and allow those children to be publicly reprimanded by a stranger? Why did they allow other children to laugh at theirs? Why did they expose their children to feelings of shame and not protect and identify themselves with the defenseless child?

The most common explanation is that parents are overburdened in bringing up their children. People may think: Since help from Saint Nicholas has become an institution, why should we not avail ourselves of it and combine the useful with a fine old tradition? The fact is, however, that Saint Nicholas, to whom this custom harks back, was a bishop who distributed food to the poor at Christmastime, but he did not combine his ministering with any pedagogic advice, nor did he threaten with the rod. It was only the pedagogic efforts of the parents that turned him into an authority that dispensed both chastisement and praise. The custom was carried so far that, as recently as in postwar Germany, Saint Nicholas sometimes appeared carrying a sack from which a child's leg protruded, leaving the reprimanded children in no doubt at all that they might be stuffed into the sack for their misdeeds.

The knowledge of these practices, among other things, helped me to understand the attitudes of today's parents. Parents who, thirty years ago, exposed their children to such a massive threat undoubtedly did not give them a chance to defend themselves against this cruelty. The children's feelings simply had to be repressed. When those children have become mothers or fathers and organize a celebration with Saint Nicholas, it is not surprising that their empathy for their sons and daughters should be blocked and that today their fear, repressed thirty years ago, should form a barrier separating them from the emotional life of their children: What I wasn't allowed to see, you mustn't see either; what didn't do me any harm won't do you any harm either.

But is it true that it didn't do them any harm, that every tradition, simply because it is dressed up in bright colors and lights, is something beautiful, good, and harmless? Through such ceremonies and through their own attitudes, the parents induce in their children the frightened certainty of being wicked, a certainty that will remain forever in their unconscious. At the same time they make it impossible for the children to recognize the cruelties being inflicted and thus cause future blindness. If thirty years earlier the mothers had not had to repress similar cruelties, their eyes and ears would today be open to the situation of their children, and we may be sure they would not permit them to be threatened, frightened, shamed, publicly laughed at, and left to cope alone, nor would they need Saint Nicholas's help for a whole year to blackmail their children and thus in turn raise them to become blackmailers. Today they would be making every effort to see that their children have less to repress and can later, as adults, assume more responsibility for their actions toward others.

Some people accuse me of exaggeration when I speak of child abuse in cases of a strict but nevertheless "normal" upbringing that has "nothing unusual" about it. Yet it is precisely the widespread nature of this type of childrearing that makes a warning imperative.

TWO

MURDERING FOR THE INNOCENCE OF THE PARENTS

THE MORE FORTHRIGHT I become in my statements, the more I learn from the reactions of others. Some reactions challenge me to further thought and precision. One such reaction has to do with the innocence of the parents. People's questions run something like this: "But surely you don't mean that parents are guilty when they mistreat their child out of desperation? After all, you've said in your own books that parents are compelled to transfer the unconscious traumas of their childhood to their own children and, as a result, mistreat, neglect, and sexually abuse them."

This kind of reasoning makes me realize that I must

now take a step that I did not dare take in my first books. I will proceed from the following very simple, virtually unquestioned perception: Any person who destroys human life renders himself guilty. This perception is in accord with our legislation, on the basis of which people are condemned to years of imprisonment; and no one can contradict my claim that this is a universal ethical principle of our society. Even when I replace "any person" by various occupational designations, the phrase does not lose validity, except perhaps for the occupations of military general and politician, these occupational groups being automatically entitled to send people to their death without having to bear the responsibility. But in times of peace, destruction of human life is not permitted and in fact is a crime that is punished. With one exception: Parents are *permitted* to destroy the lives of their children with impunity. Although this destruction is in most cases repeated in the next generation, it is far from being forbidden: All that is forbidden is to call it a scandal.

For a long time this taboo against condemning parents for their actions toward their children prevented me from clearly seeing and formulating the parents' guilt. But above all I was unable to question the actions of my own parents because of my lifelong fear of the feeling that reexperiencing my former situation might arouse: my sense of dependence on parents who had no inkling of either their child's needs or their own responsibility. For everything they did to me and failed to do for me, I always found countless explanations, so I could avoid asking: "Why did you do that to me? Why didn't you, Mother, protect me, why did you neglect me, ignore what I said? Why were your versions of me more important than the truth, why did you never tell me you were sorry, confirm my observations? Why did you blame me and punish me for something for which you were clearly the cause?"

These are all questions that as a child I was never able to ask. And later, in my adult life, of course I knew the answers, or thought I did. I told myself: My mother had a hard time as a child, repressing everything and idealizing her parents; she believed in the kind of upbringing everyone believed in then. She didn't know how I suffered because, as a result of her own history, she couldn't possibly have any sensors for a child's soul and because society bolstered her opinion that a child must be raised as an obedient robot, at the expense of its soul. Can we blame a woman who didn't know any better? Today I would say that we not only can but must blame such a parent so that we can bring to light what happens to children hour by hour and also enable the unhappy mothers to become aware of what was inflicted on them in their childhood. For the fear of blaming our parents reinforces the status quo: The ignorance and the transference of child-inimical attitudes persist. This dangerous vicious circle must be broken. It is precisely the ignorant parents who become guilty—knowledgeable parents do not.

A child who is not injured, not abused, can tell or show his mother when she enrages him or hurts him. This possibility was denied me. At the slightest resistance on my part to my mother's abuse I would have had to fear the direst punishments; and besides having to remain silent, I had to repress my memories and deaden my feelings. Of all of this my mother remained unaware; she could calmly go on applying her methods, confirm their "effectiveness," and so deem them correct and harmless. She never had to fear my reactions. She expected me to forgive her every injustice and never bear her a grudge. I complied as any child in my situation would have done; I had no alternative. My father avoided any confrontation with my mother and failed to see what was going on before his eyes. Although he didn't apply my mother's passionate pedagogic methods—on the rare occasions of his presence, he even showed me some warmth and tenderness—he never stood up for my rights. He never gave me the feeling that I had any rights at all; he never confirmed my observations and admitted my mother's cruelty.

I could never have told my father any of this as a child because I wasn't consciously aware of it. I could little afford to notice that he failed completely to assume his responsibility as a father. All I had was my comforting notion that his warm hand would protect me from every danger in life, that nothing could happen to me as long as I walked by his side with his hand holding mine.

I clung to this notion for decades to avoid having to acknowledge that the only legacy of even this hand was the good memory of a bond with another human being—with my father, who died early—but no more than that. If my father had had the courage to see what was happening to me and to defend me, my whole life would have taken a different course. I would have dared to trust my observations, to protect myself better, and not to allow myself to be damaged by ignorant people as I was by my mother. I would have dared to react to the language of my newborn children with my own instincts, instead of letting myself be intimidated by nurses who "knew better"—if as a child I had had a chance to live my feelings instead of suppressing them, to express them and stand up for my rights.

Some people react to such perceptions by arguing that each person, each parent, has an individual character and that the child can't blame his parents for their idiosyncrasies and hold them responsible for everything the child has been denied. But the parental behavior I have described has nothing to do with individual character traits. Rather, it is a common attitude toward the child for which the sole explanation is the repression of the parents' own childhood suffering, an attitude that is entirely possible to change. Every human being is at liberty to do away with his own repression and to absorb information: information on the needs of the small child, his emotional life, and the dangers inherent in the deadening of the child's feelings.

It follows that we can't evade the question of guilt, and I would like to confront the question head on rather than continue to avoid clarifying it. Although such clarification is long overdue, it may not have been possible until now, because only now are there some young people who experienced a more positive childhood and who thus need not be afraid to question the actions of their parents.

In leafing through my early books, I am struck by my constant efforts to avoid blaming parents. Again and again I pointed out that the patient has every right to experience and express his feelings of indignation, anger, and rage against his parents, yet at the same time I always added that I could not reproach the patient's parents because it was not I whom they had raised, manipulated, and hindered. After all, they had done it only to their own child. Today I see the situation differently. It is still not my aim to reproach unknown parents, but I am no longer afraid to entertain, and express, the thought that parents are guilty of crimes against their children, *even though* they act out of an inner compulsion and as an outcome of their tragic past.

I cannot imagine that any murderers or criminals do *not* act out of an inner compulsion. Nevertheless they are guilty when they destroy or mutilate human life. Although the law acknowledges "mitigating circumstances" when it can be proved that the criminal is not responsible for his actions, his motivation and personal plight do not alter the fact that one or more human lives had to be sacrificed for his situation. In contrast to court practice, I believe that every murder committed not directly in self-defense but on innocent surrogate objects is the expression of an inner compulsion, a compulsion to avenge the gross abuse, neglect, and confusion suffered during childhood and to leave the accompanying feelings in a state of repression.

Such compulsions lie behind even the cold calculations of a murderer. This can be illustrated by an example:

In 1984 I was asked for an interview by National Public Radio in Washington. Wendy Blair, the interviewer, read my books in advance, came well prepared, and seemed to have understood everything I had written. Her only problem was with my statement that no one will commit a murder when he can feel what was done to him in his childhood. Yet it was those very people in jail, I said, who were never allowed to experience the history of their childhood because it was so terrifying and because they found no one to help them. The telling of the life story of Jürgen Bartsch, from which I quote in *For Your Own Good,* was possible only because the journalist Paul Moor approached Bartsch, gained his confidence, and reawakened in him the emotions of the injured child. It is true that, in all similar cases, the murderer can recall the facts, even describe them and publish books about the abuse he suffered in his childhood, but he does so without feeling, without inner involvement, as if he were discussing the life of a stranger. Because he cannot feel, he remains under the compulsion to seek out a new victim for his suppressed, latent, and unaltered rage. Even the longest prison sentence does nothing to change this inner dynamic because the compulsion originates in childhood and can easily last sixty years or more if the murderer does not encounter someone who breathes life into his frozen emotions and thus helps at least partially to resolve the long-lasting compulsion.

I told my American interviewer that it was possible to check out my thesis by talking to prison inmates and asking them about their childhood. I was sure that they would all, without exception, report that their fathers were strict and often had to punish them, needless to say with beatings, but only because they had been bad and deserved it. I was equally sure that they would describe their mothers as loving and would cite external circumstances, such as poverty, as reasons for the cruelties they suffered.

Although my interviewer had difficulty accepting the mechanism of denial as an explanation for crime, she told me that statistics confirmed my statements. Those statistics showed that ninety percent of inmates in American prisons had been abused as children. I told her I was convinced that it was not ninety but a full one hundred percent. It was simply that the remaining ten percent were not yet able to admit it: They were not merely repressing their feelings but also denying the facts.

It is possible, of course, that the first abuses were inflicted not by the parents but by the inhuman child-delivery practices in our hospitals. This cause is hard to pinpoint in individual cases, and a baby seriously traumatized during birth or isolated from human contact in an incubator may at a very early stage become a "difficult child" who hardly can get the love he will need to overcome the trauma. But it is absolutely unthinkable that a human being who, from the start, is given love, tenderness, closeness, orientation, respect, honesty, and protection by adults should later become a murderer.

"Can the explanation really be so simple?" asked my interviewer. It is very simple, yet most people seem to have a problem with it because access to this simple truth remains blocked by the pain experienced in their own childhood. They prefer to believe in theories that sound very complicated but have the advantage of sparing them pain. As a result, millions of prison inmates are deprived of help. They serve their time senselessly: Nothing in them is changed, and a machinery is kept in motion that ensures, among other things, that the guilt of the prisoners' parents remains undiscovered.

"But what happens," my interviewer wanted to know, "when a person in therapy finds out what his parents have done to him? Isn't it possible that he might want to kill his parents? I mean, that the reawakened feeling is no protection against murder?" No, I told her, it is possible that this person might wish to do it, but he won't, for two reasons. First, through reawakened feelings, he will sense the awakening of life within him and won't want to jeopardize that life. Second, feelings that can be associated with childhood experiences can change over time and make way for new feelings. The anger directed at parents remains unchanged as long as we cannot feel it, because we fear this anger, feel guilty about it, and are afraid of the parents' revenge. Once this fear has been experienced with all its attendant circumstances, and its ramifications have been understood, we are no longer compelled to feel guilty about something done by others. This liberation reduces the anger.

I wasn't quite sure when we parted whether my interviewer had found in my explanations the answers she was looking for, but the completed cassette she sent me showed that she had understood me correctly. Into our conversation she had woven interviews with victims of abuse and one interview, which had been stored for years in the archives of her radio station, with a man who had killed three hundred and sixty women. The journalist who interviewed the murderer had initially been struck by the fact that the man talked about his murders quite unemotionally, but the significance of this absence of emotion became clear to the journalist only through the strength of my arguments. In reply to questions, the murderer stated that his mother had been a prostitute and had hit him "whenever [he] didn't stay out of her way." On a few occasions she had almost killed him. When he was born she had wanted a girl, not a boy, and until he was seven years old he was forced to wear girl's clothes and to keep his hair long. When a teacher cut his hair, his mother was so furious she almost beat the teacher to death. What had he felt while committing the murders? Nothing, said the prisoner. He set out from his house each morning with the purpose of killing a woman, as if he were going out to do a day's work. Could

29

it be that his harsh childhood had something to do with these murders? the journalist wanted to know. "Oh no," replied the prisoner with total conviction, and for the first time with a trace of emotion. "I cannot blame my mother for what happened to me."

This man had repressed his past so thoroughly that he had never in his life had a dream. He was fourteen when he first murdered a girl, one his own age. Presumably he wished to destroy the girl whom his mother had wanted instead of him. He murdered out of the simple and understandable despair resulting from his realization that he could never win his mother's love because he was a boy and not a girl. Had his mother expected something else of him—something attainable—he might have managed to live up to her wishes, but this was a chance that life had not given him. A child will do anything to win his mother's love because he cannot live without that love. So this child, who received only hatred from a mother who might, he believed, have so much love to offer, sought a way to obtain her love. Perhaps the boy felt compelled to kill the girl merely to gain attention. We know nothing of that. Only he could have told us, provided he had had the possibility of feeling, of weeping, of dreaming. But he hadn't. His soul was immured. Murder was its only language.

Who, then, is guilty of the death of those three hundred and sixty women? The adult murderer, of course. But not only he. Once we are prepared to look at the surrounding circumstances we can no longer say that his mother is without guilt. The murderer says that his mother cannot be blamed for what happened to him, and society agrees with him. In my opinion this mother made her son a murderer, even if the son doesn't know it, even if society and the mother herself don't know it or don't want to know it. It is this very lack of awareness that is so dangerous. To prevent future crimes, the danger of this ignorance must be clearly recognized.

This conclusion is so obvious, so banal, that one would hardly expect any serious resistance to the necessary task of enlightenment. Yet that resistance, especially among those parents who are most urgently in need of such enlightenment, is intense. Why? After all, one would think it would be helpful for parents to find out more about how they unconsciously injure their children so they can avoid such behavior in the future. The fact is, though, that the parents most likely to benefit from proper information about the emotional life of the child are those who were not traumatized as children. Unfortunately they form a minority, for since childhood most parents have been in an emotional trap, waiting only for a chance to discharge their unconscious, pent-up anger. They can find no other door out of this trap than their own children, for only those children may, under the guise of childrearing and with impunity, be beaten, scolded, and humiliated just as their parents once were.

The tragedy is that a person caught in a trap and seeing only one door can't resist using that door. He will remain blind and deaf to any sensible information as long as the door is not closed once and for all through appropriate legislation. If it were a legal offense to act out one's rage against one's own parents on one's own children, other ways out of the trap would have to be sought, and parents would find them. Certainly, anguish over what has been inflicted on oneself is unavoidable, but it has been shown that such anguish can be healing, not destructive.

31

If a mother could feel how she is injuring her child, she would be able to discover how she was once injured herself and so could rid herself of her compulsion to repeat the past. Yet education and religion forbid her to feel what was inflicted on her. This refusal to acknowledge the consequences of former harm and injury to the child permeates our society and is reinforced by religious teachings. For thousands of years, all religious institutions have exhorted the faithful to respect their parents. These exhortations would be entirely unnecessary if people grew up in an atmosphere of love and respect, for then they would react naturally to all that they received. But when a person has no reason to respect his parents, he must, it seems, be coerced into doing so. The dangerous effect of such coercion is that any criticism of parents is called a sin and results in strong feelings of guilt. Because religions teach that parents, even if already dead, must be shielded under any circumstances, they do so at the cost of the parents' children. That this teaching is called moral only magnifies the scandal.

Future life is sacrificed to secure a forced respect for people who, having grossly misused their power when their children were small and trusting, do not deserve this respect. Nevertheless, almost every culture adheres to the commandment to respect one's parents. Over and over again, Indians, Vietnamese, Chinese, Arabs, and Africans have told me the same stories: "We had to be beaten to learn respect for our parents. Whatever they said or did was always sacred." Some of them add: "We, too, must raise our children to have respect for us; otherwise they'll turn into vandals." Only in rare cases do they realize that by beating their children they are—just like white people—laying dynamite and generating vandalism. A black psychology student in a group in London once told me, "From the very beginning I was physically, psychically, and sexually abused." "How did you come to realize this?" I asked him. "It was your books that made me aware of it, and now I see it all around me. But everyone, blacks as well as whites, tells me that what I see is not true. Our parents claim to have learned cruelty from the whites and deny their own parents' contribution."

"He who spares the rod hates his son, but he who loves him is diligent to discipline him," we read in Proverbs. This so-called wisdom is still so widespread today that we can often hear: A slap given in love does a child no harm. Even Kafka, who had a very fine ear for spurious undertones, is supposed to have said, according to a witness, "Love often has the face of violence." I consider it unlikely that the witness quoted Kafka correctly, but Kafka forced himself, as we all do, to regard cruelty as love.

Can there be such a thing as cruelty out of love? If people weren't accustomed to the biblical injunction from childhood, it would soon strike them as the untruth it is. Cruelty is the opposite of love, and its traumatic effect, far from being reduced, is actually reinforced if it is presented as a sign of love. In a book by the American television personality Phil Donahue, published in 1985, the following passage occurs:

So what is a parent to do? Does all this mean you should never spank your kids? You don't want them to grow up stealing hubcaps; but you also don't want them to grow up undisciplined. Is there any way to punish a child without leaving emotional scars? Are children so sensitive to physical punishment that the slightest slap on the wrist constitutes traumatic "abuse" and will ensure that the child grows up either delin-

33

quent or hopelessly neurotic? Is it possible to discipline a child physically without suffering from terminal guilt yourself if you do?

Not all behavioral experts agree with [Alice] Miller that punishment, even if administered in the context of a loving relationship, is inevitably destructive. Harvard's Jerome Kagan, for example, thinks children are capable of accepting punishment without developing propensities toward violence as adults. He believes that, except in extreme cases of abuse, parental behavior is not as important as how the child interprets that behavior. "If the child interprets the physical punishment as unfair," rather than as a reflection of the "parent's desire to help him become a productive adult," says Kagan, "then you get delinquency, crime, drugs, and so on."

In fact, Kagan thinks that many scientists exaggerate the role of parents in causing violent behavior in their children. Although he's foursquare against parental beatings and sexual abuse, he has a lot of confidence in the ability of the human animal to survive a traumatic childhood and become a responsible member of society. The typical response of parents who discover their children engaging in some antisocial behavior is guilt. They wonder, "What did I do wrong?" According to Kagan, the answer is probably nothing. He thinks it's simplistic to assume, every time a youngster snatches a purse from an old lady, that his mother didn't love him enough.

Although Donahue's discussion ostensibly proceeds from the question of which parental behavior might exert a traumatizing and lasting effect on the child, and although it would appear to give priority to concern for the child, the second paragraph shows that basically it is concerned only with liberating parents from justified guilt feelings. They are assured that their actions pose no danger: The child will suffer no harm if he knows that he is being tormented out of "love" and "for his own good." This kind of reassurance that relies on untruths is based on the statements of "experts" quoted here and, I need hardly say, corresponds to the wishes of all parents who are not prepared to question their own behavior.

But might not there be a different way, other than reassurances? Might not one explain to the parents, in all honesty and frankness, *why* they traumatize their children? Not all of them would stop tormenting their children, but some would. We can be certain, however, that they would *not* stop if they were told, as were their own parents thirty years earlier, that one slap more or less does no harm, provided they love the child. Although this phrase contains a contradiction, it can continue to be handed down because we are used to it. Love and cruelty are mutually exclusive. No one ever slaps a child out of love but rather because in similar situations, when one was defenseless, one was slapped and then compelled to interpret it as a sign of love. This inner confusion prevailed for thirty or forty years and is passed on to one's own child. That's all. To purvey this confusion to the child as truth leads to new confusions that, although examined in detail by experts, are still confusions. If, on the other hand, one can admit one's errors to the child and apologize for a lack of self-control, no confusions are created.

If a mother can make it clear to a child that at that particular moment when she slapped him her love for him deserted her and she was dominated by other feelings that had nothing to do with the child, the child can keep a clear head, feel respected, and not be disoriented in his relationship to his mother. While it is true that love for a child cannot be commanded, each of us is free to decide to refrain from hypocrisy. I don't know whether hypocrisy exists in the animal world; at least I have never heard of a young animal growing up with the idea that it has to be tormented almost to death so that one day it may become a "decent and disciplined animal." Kagan's well-meant but naive trust in the ability of the "human animal" to survive a traumatic childhood unscathed ignores completely the potent, destructive, and disastrous nature of the traumas inflicted on the child. Many comparisons between human and animal aggression also ignore the fact that, in light of humans' destructive atomic power and *readiness* to destroy (as documented by Hitler and Stalin), all the bared animal teeth in the world are bound to appear downright innocuous. Is it possible that Harvard professors don't know this? Absolutely. If they derived their trust in the harmless nature of childhood traumas from the convictions of their grandmothers, they will learn nothing from facts because this trust clearly remains unshaken throughout their lives. But in view of the great confusions they are causing, in view of the dangerous hypocrisy they support, this trust is anything but harmless, since it is precisely the consequences of those universally ignored childhood traumas that threaten the world today.

THREE

THE WICKED CHILD

---

*A Favorite Fairy Tale
of Scientists*

CONGENITAL BLINDNESS is in most cases an irreversible fate. But the emotional blindness that I am about to describe is not congenital. It is the consequence of a repression of feelings and memories that renders a person unable to see certain sets of circumstances. This blindness is not irreversible, since everyone can later decide to put an end to his repression. At that moment he needs help from other people, and this he can find if he is genuinely determined to confront the truth.

Whether or not the individual seizes this chance depends largely on the nature of his childhood: Did it resemble a totalitarian regime in which the only authority was the state police? Or was the child once given the chance to experience something other than cruelty so that, in the present situation as an adult, he can fall back on this happy experience?

To encounter one's own history not only puts an end to the blindness hitherto displayed toward the child within oneself but also reduces the blockage of thought and feeling. I will return to this point later, but now I offer some examples of how this blindness functions and how it influences human thought.

In the American weekly *Newsday Magazine* a few years ago, the writer Ann Jones devoted several pages to examining the question of what can induce a woman to kill her child. A recent murder of an eight-month-old infant had prompted general speculations. The author starts by describing the situation: A young woman is alone at home with her three-year-old son and eight-month-old daughter. She has just had an unpleasant telephone conversation with her father and now wants to tell her sister about it, but the baby constantly interferes with the conversation and never stops screaming. Unable to hear her sister's voice, the mother becomes more and more desperate and suddenly starts hitting the baby with the receiver until the infant is silent. Thus she becomes a child murderer, although she did not deliberately kill the baby. She merely wanted to get rid of the intolerable screaming.

The author describes the sufferings of this woman in childhood. Her father was an alcoholic and would often run around the apartment brandishing a knife and threatening to kill his two young daughters. He beat them regularly and abused them sexually when they were quite small. Once he dragged the girl from her sleep and hung her by her nightgown from a nail in the wall, leaving her there for three hours. The parents were having a quarrel, and the mother deserted the father at the very time the girl was hanging on the wall.

These examples are enough to show what tortures the present child murderer was herself exposed to as a child. Moreover, in later life she was never allowed to do what she really wanted: she had many unwanted pregnancies and was never allowed to have an abortion. The role of mother was forced on her, by her immature partners as well as by medical authorities, and eventually she killed her baby. It is significant that she committed murder while trying vainly to articulate her terrible distress. She was hoping to obtain relief on the telephone, presumably trying to tell her sister about their father's outrageous remarks over the phone, but the baby's screaming made this impossible. It forced on her the mother role for which at that moment she was least prepared, once again stifling the articulation of her distress, as other situations had so often done before. But here, with the weakest creature at hand, she could "defend" herself.

Later, in prison, she gave birth to another child, and again there was no one within reach who might have searched with her for the roots of this senseless cycle of birth and destruction. Even the magazine article fails to do this. The initially described childhood is quickly forgotten, and a whole series of circumstances from her adult life is put forward as cause for this murder: partners, men, poverty—all these factors are to blame when a mother kills her baby, the article finally concludes. Various experts are quoted, various theories advanced, various suggestions made, and research projects are called for that will at last get down to the question of how society causes certain women to kill their children.

What was so obvious at the beginning of the article has by its end been virtually obscured. Why? For a very simple reason, the reason that was presumably also the determining factor in Freud's suppression of the truth in 1897 (discussed in more detail in the next chapter). Let us try to imagine that as a child, hanging from the wall for three hours by our nightgown, we are abandoned by our mother and left totally at the mercy of a rampaging father, and let us go on to imagine what emotions this would arouse in us. We balk at imagining this, for such an attempt recalls similar situations of which we don't wish to be reminded at any price. What can a child do when she is left so utterly alone with her panic, her impotent fury, her despair and anguish? The child must not even cry, much less scream, if she doesn't want to be killed. The only way she can get rid of these emotions is to repress them. But repression is a perfidious fairy who will supply help at the moment but will eventually exact a price for this help. The impotent fury comes to life again when the girl's own child is born, and at last the anger can be discharged—once again at the expense of a defenseless creature.

When such a child must consume all her capability and energy for the required labor of repression; when, in addition, she has never known what it is to be loved and protected by someone, this child will eventually also be incapable of protecting herself and organizing her life in a meaningful and productive manner. This child will continue to torment herself in destructive relationships, taking up with irresponsible partners and suffering from them; but she is unlikely to be able to grasp that the origin of all this suffering is to be found in her own parents and others involved in her upbringing. That former labor of repression to ensure survival renders such an insight impossible, contrary now to the interests of the adult who was once that child. If, to survive, a child is required to ignore certain things, the chances are that she will be required to continue to ignore those things for the rest of her life.

The life-saving function of repression in childhood is transformed in adulthood into a life-destroying force. If the mother who ended up as a child murderer could have consciously experienced her hatred for her father, she would not have had to repress her childhood feelings and would not have become a murderer. She would have known at whom her hatred was directed when she became so desperate on the phone, and she would not have made her own child pay the price for it. The blindness that was once essential turned her into a murderer, and the blindness of society contributes to this woman's inability to find help. For even after many years in prison or many years of educationally oriented therapy, she is still not rid of her latent hatred for her father and of her fear of being a screaming child who must be punished. She is in danger of repeating her crime, of having repeatedly to eliminate the screaming child she was never allowed to be, as long as society—including therapists—is governed by the fear of questioning the actions of parents.

Much of what we have learned from earliest childhood, and continue hearing in later life, is sustained by this fear. Entwined with the fear is the idea that the child is basically something wicked that by means of our culture we should tame and turn into something better. A whole series of such ideas exists, ideas that are constantly

41

mocked by reality yet are not easy to change, justifying as they do our system of childrearing. Theories, often quite complex, are built up on such ideas, theories that students learn at every university and years later teach as professors, although these theories have been proved to be untrue. In *Thou Shalt Not Be Aware*, I have demonstrated how precisely Freud's "drive" theory and Melanie Klein's theory of the cruel infant coincide with the traditional pedagogic view of the child. That which Martin Luther postulated four hundred years ago is still accepted today; thus, for instance, the psychoanalyst Edward Glover writes:

Expressing these technical discoveries in social terms we can say that the perfectly normal infant is almost completely egocentric, greedy, dirty, violent in temper, destructive in habit, profoundly sexual in purpose, aggrandizing in attitude, devoid of all but the most primitive reality sense, without conscience or moral feeling, whose attitude to society (as represented by the family) is opportunist, inconsiderate, domineering and sadistic. And when we come to consider the criminal type labeled psychopathic it will be apparent that many of these characteristics can under certain circumstances persist into adult life. In fact, judged by adult social standards the normal baby is for all practical purposes a born criminal.

When I oppose this thesis of the cruel child, the alleged sexuality of the child is often pointed out to me. Without the moral attitude of "poisonous pedagogy," which I describe in *For Your Own Good*, such a line of reasoning would be unthinkable for it assumes that sexuality is something bad and culpable. So far, psychoanalysis has not seemed to free itself from such evaluations. Although the assertion of infantile sexuality was declared the principal dogma of psychoanalysis, it is not clear what definition of sexuality this assertion is based on. The literature of psychoanalysis contains examples of very heterogeneous phenomena, such as childish curiosity and sensuality and the desire for physical closeness, for stimulation by stroking, for caressing and soothing, for gentle touching, for the physical warmth of another person, and for numerous pleasure experiences in the child's own body, including in the genitals. Yet all this doesn't amount to sexuality, even though adults who were once raised with coldness and physical deprivation may like to call it that. In Sigmund Freud's day, childish autoeroticism was punished with extreme severity, and the touching of the genitals was countered with threats of castration because adults projected feelings of their own "impurity" onto the child and punished him for their own forbidden fantasies. However, this is not nearly reason enough to equate childish autoeroticism, sensuality, and curiosity with sexuality.

Sexuality is the copulative urge of human beings, who do not receive their hormonal directive until puberty. Proceeding from this biological definition, it is logical that I do not find this sexuality in children. It goes without saying that sexual abuse of children leaves its mark on its victims. Thus an abused child can simulate "sexual" behavior so as not to lose the regard of the adult. The result is a distorted picture. I have long been preoccupied with the question of why the plight of sexually abused children and their behavior are constantly being cited, in courtrooms as well as in psychoanalytic practice, as proof of their guilt. One reason is that adults unload their "impure" sexuality by ascribing it to the child through projection.

43

Even if the copulation urge were already active in newborn infants—which, of course, is utter nonsense—why should that be regarded as culpable? Sexuality is a natural urge that can't be held responsible if some people resort to it to impair or destroy the lives of others. Such people become culpable, not because they succumb to the copulation urge but because in their history this urge was coupled with other factors such as cruelty, humiliation, and the exercise of power and because, on the basis of this history, they act destructively. When they include sexuality in their destructive acts, sexuality cannot be blamed for those acts. Taking the example of Jürgen Bartsch, I demonstrated in *For Your Own Good* how a person who has been tormented in childhood becomes culpable and how misleading it is to hold his sexuality and alleged "uncontrolled drives" responsible. A small child cannot be cruel for the simple reason that he is defenseless and unable as yet to take revenge on others for the torments he has suffered—except perhaps on small animals. The child has not yet the power to destroy human lives, even though, of course, he can—and must—harbor murderous thoughts and vengeful desires in his imagination.

A young pediatric analyst, who practices according to Melanie Klein's method, once told me: "You obviously have no children of your own. Otherwise you would know that children are not, as you describe them, innocent, but have cruel imaginations. This can be observed even in the way an infant smacks its mother." I didn't immediately tell this young analyst that I am the mother of two children; instead I asked her what she meant by "smack." She described a child who in a frenzy hit his mother's face with his hands—with his fists even, she

44

said. Although she herself had no children, she had observed such behavior on several occasions; moreover, mothers of children who were her patients had reported the same behavior to her. I tried to query her certainty: This smacking, I argued, might also be a harmless game; it depends on how the mother sees it. It is only if the mother feels humiliated and beaten, if she confuses the child with her own parents and resorts to pedagogic measures, that what began as playful behavior on the part of the child can turn into frustration and assume destructive traits. The child then feels misunderstood, and the only way he can express his frustration is by hitting the mother's face with his fists. If I describe such a situation to someone who hasn't been trained for ten years in the Kleinian theory, I am immediately understood. But this analyst looked at me with suspicion as she said, "Melanie Klein spent all her life working with children, and her theories were based on her observations."

That's precisely the point: What kind of eyes are doing the observing? A mother sees her frenzied, screaming child and is firmly convinced that children must be disciplined. After all, that is what she learned from her mother, and those early lessons are extremely effective. Melanie Klein observed her child and the other children in her practice against the background of her own upbringing and apparently couldn't see beyond what she had learned in her own youth from her mother. Since time immemorial, gynecologists, nurses, and parents have observed screaming newborn infants and have likewise remained blind to the fact that those screams are the expression of psychic distress and are altogether avoidable.

My assertion that the infant is innocent has nothing to

do with romantic idealization, nor is it derived from this or that philosophical evaluation. It stems rather from the reality of the child's situation: A baby is defenseless and as yet bears no responsibility for others; as yet, he owes nobody anything. But this fact does not contradict the frequent observation that children can behave very cruelly, just as cruelly as they have been treated by others. Erin Pizzey, the founder of shelters for battered women and children, reports that there are even some three-year-olds who cannot tussle playfully but fight each other as if to kill. In their behavior these children reflect in every detail the brutality they experienced at home and reveal unmistakably where they learned their destructive behavior.

I am often asked by worried parents whether children are learning cruelty from television. In my view a child who harbors no pent-up rage will show no interest in brutal and sadistic TV programs. However, brutal programs are avidly absorbed by children who have never been allowed to defend themselves against overt or subtle tormenting at home or who, for other reasons, can never articulate their feelings—for example, to spare a threatened parent. So they can satisfy their secret longings for revenge by identifying with what they see on TV. These children already carry within them the seeds of future destructiveness. Whether or not this destructiveness will erupt depends largely on whether life offers them more than violence: in other words, whether witnesses willing to rescue them cross their path. What is important to understand is that the child learns cruelty not by watching TV but always by suffering and repressing.

The school of cruelty is often coupled with sexual

abuse. When, for instance, a twenty-year-old man masturbates a five-year-old boy, the destructive components of gratification of desire are imposed on the child by the adult. The child will never free himself from this type of gratification and, as an adult, will be subject to the unconscious compulsion to avenge on another child, in some form or other, the rape he once experienced. Thus destructiveness, with all its attendant rationalizations, is taught, learned, and disguised.

It is only from adults that an unloved child learns to hate or torment and to disguise these feelings with lies and hypocrisy. That is why, when the child has grown up, he or she will say that children require norms and disciplining: This lie provides access to adult society, a lie that permeates all pedagogy and, to this day, psychoanalysis. The young child knows no lies, is prepared to take at their face value such words as *truth, love,* and *mercy* as heard in religious instruction in school. Only on finding out that his naiveté is cause for ridicule does the child learn to dissemble. The child's upbringing teaches him the patterns of the destructive behavior that will later be interpreted by experts as the result of an innate destructive drive. Anyone daring to question this assertion will be smiled at as being naive, as if that person had never come in contact with children and didn't know "how they can get on your nerves." For at least since the days of Sigmund Freud, it has been known in "progressive" circles that children come into this world with a death drive and might kill us all if we didn't ward off "the first indications."

In the early 1980s a professor asked me for an interview for her journal, the subject of which would be my critique of psychoanalysis. I was unable at the time to answer her questions, which I received in writing, but I promised to deal with them in my next book. I propose to do this here because they represent an attitude I often come across: Although the people asking such questions make an effort to acquire new insights, they have no intention of giving up the old lessons received from their parents, lessons later reaffirmed by various theories at university. One of the many questions I was asked by the professor went like this: "When you postulate the child as being innocent, you appear to deny that he is subject to his desires. You show how impotent, alienated, and dependent the child is, how much at the mercy of the will of adults. But, after all, the child is not without desires, without fantasies, without transference."

Why should a child be considered culpable simply because he is "subject to desires, fantasies, and transferences"? It goes without saying that a child, even a newborn infant, is a bundle of needs, but it would never have occurred to anyone to call this guilt if our parents hadn't perceived our needs and desires as tiresome demands. We have learned to feel guilty about our desires and needs, and we introduce this fundamental perception into our theories. This confusion is implicit in the question I just quoted. A child is not really permitted to be a subject; he must remain the object of pedagogy. The fact that, in addition, the child is deemed guilty in this role should not surprise us in the least. There is nothing that can't be imputed to a child and, tragically, the labels we place on the child can remain effective for a lifetime. The child who was once accused believes throughout life in his guilt and wickedness because he has desires and fantasies. And later, in adult life, this belief prevents him from seeing that "wicked" and difficult children have been made into that.

Most people show not the slightest interest in the question of why a child has turned out this way or that. When the causes are pointed out to them—the brutality of the father, the inner absorption of the mother—they say: That's no excuse for stealing; everyone has had problems in childhood, but that's far from turning him into a criminal. The fact that differences in development can be accounted for by the degree of affection received by children does not interest them. So there remains only one question for them: How can I discipline my child, how must I punish him so that he will grow up into a decent human being and not lie, not steal, not run away? One often hears people say: Children who are spoiled and given anything they ask for at home will steal if required to work; one must accustom them to the idea that they get nothing without working for it, one must accustom them at an early age to the fact that life is hard, one must not give them everything they want, even if one could, one must set them limits, one must, one must. . . .

When I question such views and say, for example, The child must have the freedom to set *us* limits when we demand too much of him, mistreat or humiliate him, I meet with great astonishment. I am asked: Do you have any children of your own? Don't you know how wicked children can be? You idealize children, as if you had never seen a difficult child.

Of course I have, even in psychiatric clinics where they resisted the most ingenious pedagogic methods—for instance, by not speaking, by refusing food, by tearing out their hair—because there was no one around who was

genuinely interested in their torment and able to understand their pain. Everyone made an effort to discipline
these children, to teach them something positive such as
reading, writing, talking, eating, but no one wanted to
find out about the tragedy of their existence. Whenever I
asked about this in my discussions with doctors and
nurses, I was struck by how little the caregivers knew
about the children's history and family situation. But
what they did tell me was enough for me to realize the
psychic terrorization the children had undergone, yet
the doctors never realized this themselves. For what I call
"hell" is for them still the most normal thing in the
world, and they go on to say: But then everybody could
become psychotic, autistic, mute, for there are plenty of
people who have had similar experiences. They fall back
on innate biological factors, which they try to mitigate, as
best they can, with education and medication.

Such attempts, well meaning and honest though they
may be, involve the danger of further traumatizing and
confusing the child who, despite all those efforts, will still
not be understood as long as cruelty toward children is
not fully recognized.

Some opinions are passed on without question from
generation to generation, with such conviction that no
one takes the trouble to challenge them. And not only
because of the fear of reprisals: Very often the threat of
reprisals doesn't even arise because the traditional opinions are actually believed to be correct. Let me illustrate
this by an example.

I am frequently asked by various clinics to give lec-
tures. Rather than carry on a monologue, I try to get the
hospital staff into a conversation during which those
present can ask me their questions. Again and again in

such discussions I encounter certain adherents of psychoanalysis whose attitude seems to me typical. They praise my work and appreciate my "efforts on behalf of abused children," but as a rule they completely fail to grasp the implications of what I have been saying as applied to their theory. Oblivious to it all, they end by citing their credo: that there is such a thing as fantasizing incest, that the newborn infant comes into the world not innocent but with destructive drives, and that in cases of incest there are no violations but only "interactions" between child and adult.

I recently had such an experience with the head of a clinic who is considered by his colleagues to be a man of empathy and who at least does not prescribe harmful medication. The nurses on his station told me about the terrible traumas to which the young psychotic and autistic patients had been exposed. So the staff were aware. The head of the clinic was also aware of the facts. Nevertheless he failed to see any connections. He hadn't yet realized that, given our present knowledge about child abuse, the Freudian theories have become untenable. How could he have? He is too busy to read newspaper reports of child abuse; besides, they don't interest him. He still regards what he learned twenty or thirty years ago as correct, even writes books about it; he sees patients, heads a work team. How can he be expected to question what he learned if he has never tried to link in his mind the theories he has learned, his practical work, and the reports about child abuse?

Reactions to new insights reflect not only training but also the tragedy of unequal chances: A loved child receives the gift of love and with it that of knowledge and innocence. It is a gift that will provide him with orienta-

51

tion for his whole life. An injured child lacks everything because he lacks love. He doesn't know what love is, constantly confuses crime with good deeds and mendacity with truth, and hence will continue to be subject to new confusions.

This confusion also became apparent to me in a discussion of an actual case among experts: A woman who had not been subject to achievement pressure in her childhood and had been much loved took into her home a nine-year-old autistic boy, whom she later adopted. She was able to give him plenty of warmth and physical contact, react to him positively, confirm his feelings, sense his needs, pick up his signals, and eventually understand them too. In her arms the boy learned to show emotions, to experience the anger at what had been done to him in the past, and to discover love. He developed into a healthy, intelligent, very lively, and candid youth.

I recounted this history to a group of experts in the field of autism. The doctors among them said that autism was an incurable neurophysiological disease and that the history in this case showed that the boy had not been suffering from autism; in other words, there had been a wrong diagnosis. The psychologists, family therapists, and analysts said that this history was probably a crude simplification, for they knew many cases in which years of psychotherapy had brought about no change in autistic patients (which, incidentally, I am perfectly willing to believe). They went on to say that such a history could be of no help to parents of autistic children; on the contrary, it would give them guilt feelings because not all parents were in a position to devote that much love and time to their child. The parents usually had several children, had to earn a living, and, after all, they were only human. I said it seemed to me irrelevant whether a parent acquired guilt feelings when it was a matter of uncovering such an important truth.

The history of the nine-year-old boy confirmed something I had long suspected: A child's autism is a response to his environment, sometimes the last possible response open to a child. Whether autism is curable depends on the extent to which the people in a new environment can become aware of the truth of the child's past. The reaction of those experts showed how difficult it is to find such people. Their resistance prevented them from realizing how greatly this boy's history could help us in our dealings with children.

Later, after many years, I heard of similar though still rare cases of autistic children being cured. A technique was developed, the "holding" technique, aimed at the need of the lost, lonely, alienated child to be held. Unfortunately this technique was once again coupled with pedagogy, and that is where I see its great danger. If the mother has gained the child's trust by holding him and proceeds to place pedagogic demands on him, the child will do anything in his power not to lose his mother's affection again. It has actually been shown that children treated with this technique do brilliantly in school. But since I wrote my first book, in 1979, I have known that this is not necessarily a genuine cure. The mother's complete physical and psychic devotion to the autistic child can no doubt work miracles, provided she refrains from making pedagogic demands; otherwise she will create the drama of the gifted child—the very thing the child was warding off with his autism.

FOUR

THEORIES AS A PROTECTIVE SHIELD

THE OPINIONS most hotly defended are the very ones
that are *not* correct yet conform to our childrearing system. The dogmatizing of these false claims protects the
abused individual from a painful awakening. The same
function is also fulfilled by the Freudian theories of infantile sexuality, the Oedipus complex, and the death
instinct. Freud originally discovered, in the treatments
partially conducted under hypnosis, that all his patients,
both female and male, had been abused children and
recounted their histories in the language of symptoms.
After reporting his discovery in psychiatric circles, he
found himself completely shunned because none of his

fellow psychiatrists was prepared to share the findings with him. Freud could not bear this isolation for long. A few months later, in 1897, he described his patients' reports on sexual abuse as sheer fantasies attributable to their instinctual wishes. Humanity's briefly disturbed sleep could now be resumed.

Everyone who is confronted with child abuse and observes in others the extent to which experiences of abuse are repressed and denied must feel profoundly shaken, for he is bound to wonder: What was it like in my case? If obvious victims of the worst kind of abuse can deny their experiences so completely, how can I be sure that my memory doesn't deceive me? This question also arose for Freud, when he was still open to questions and not armed against them with theories. A number of hypotheses emerged, among others a massive accusation of his father, as appears in one of his letters to Fliess:

Unfortunately, my own father was one of these perverts and is responsible for the hysteria of my brother (all of whose symptoms are identifications) and those of several younger sisters. The frequency of this circumstance often makes me wonder.

Everyone can discover for himself what fears such accusations against his own father would arouse in him. How much more dangerous such thoughts must have been a hundred years ago. Yet perhaps Freud would have found the strength to test his hypothesis about his father if there had been one single person to support him. But his closest confidant, Wilhelm Fliess, had no idea what to make of Freud's discovery. Fliess's son, Robert Fliess, however, later became a psychiatrist and analyst and published three books containing some very revealing material on sexual abuse by parents of their own children. It took Robert Fliess many decades to find out that, at the age of two, he had been sexually abused by his father and that this incident coincided with Freud's renunciation of the truth. In his book Robert Fliess made his personal history public because he was convinced that his father had deterred Freud from further developing the trauma theory. That theory would have inevitably caused Wilhelm Fliess guilt feelings, so his son believes. How far this assumption is correct is difficult for an outsider to judge.

Apart from this explanation of Freud's betrayal of the truth in 1897, there are several others. What they all have in common is that individual aspects of Freud's private life are made responsible for his fateful step.

It may be that all these factors played a role of greater or lesser significance and that they even support one another. But their potency is based on the commandment "Thou shalt not be aware," which to this day forbids us to see what parents inflict on their children. Despite the effectiveness of this commandment, there have already been some therapists, such as Sandor Ferenczi and Robert Fliess, who tried to free themselves. But without casting doubt on one's own parents, without the intense pain caused by an abandonment of illusions, without the help and support of others who would also like to overcome their blindness or have already succeeded in doing so, this independence and clarity of vision are almost impossible to achieve. So it is really not surprising (although it is disastrous) that ninety years ago Sigmund Freud should have yielded to that commandment, to his fear, and to his repression.

Wilhelm Reich later did the same thing when he developed a theory intended to help him ward off the pain of the very young child he once was who had constantly been sexually exploited. Instead of feeling the hurt of being victimized by trusted adults and of having to accept his victimization submissively, Wilhelm Reich maintained throughout his life, to the point of becoming psychotic: I wanted that myself, I needed that, every child needs that!

Yet our sympathy for Reich and Freud must not prevent us from seeing that with his drive theory Freud has inflicted great harm on humanity. Instead of taking his personal plight seriously, he sought shelter from it behind theories. By going even further, by founding a school and dogmatizing his theses, he institutionalized the denial that endowed the lies of pedagogy with alleged scientific legitimacy. For the Freudian dogmas corresponded to the widespread notion that the child is by nature wicked and bad and must be trained by adults to be good. This perfect consensus with pedagogy in turn bestowed on psychoanalysis society's high esteem, and for a long time the falsity of its dogmas went unnoticed.

The pedagogic protection of these theories is so great that even the feminist movement failed to see through it. Thus it became possible for the drive theory to be regarded even by committed women as progress rather than denial of child abuse.

Many people still believe that Freud is not to be blamed if certain psychoanalysts are blind to reality, are imprecise, and disclaim responsibility, for after all Freud was a brilliant discoverer, wasn't he? Similar claims are made for C. G. Jung—the fathers are idealized at the expense of the "sons" and "daughters." But it is not current practitioners who invented psychoanalysis—it was invented by the "father," and by dogmatizing the denial of the truth Freud made it difficult for the "sons" and "daughters" to use their eyes and ears. They had little chance of refuting his claims on the basis of their experiences, since a dogma cannot be refuted. A dogma lives on its followers' fear of losing their group affiliation. It is from this fear that the dogma derives its power, and it is due to this power that people "work" every day, for thirty or forty years, with victims of child abuse without even being aware that they are working with such victims, with the result that even the patients cannot penetrate to their own truth. Since the game of words, associations, and speculations takes its orientation from the patients' "fantasies" and not from the actual childhood background, the results lack the necessary accuracy and cannot be tested.

In my opinion, the founder of psychoanalysis himself must be held responsible for the dogmatizing of the drive theory. If someone describes the renunciation of reality as a great scientific advance and founds a school that supports its students in their blindness, this ceases to be a private matter. It amounts to a violation of the interests of humanity, even when performed unconsciously. But that, after all, is the precondition for violations: They would not exist if people were fully aware of their situation, their history, and their responsibility.

In the last few years I have learned more than ever about the situation of the child in our society and about the blockages in the thinking and feeling of psychoanalytically trained persons. These blockages often result in patients being subjected to lengthy treatments that cement the blame that had been leveled at them as children, a process that can scarcely lead to anything but depressions. The most successful means of escaping such chronic depressions is to enter the profession of psychoanalysis oneself; this permits a continuation of the cementing process by using theories that protect one from the truth—but now, of course, at the expense of others.

Psychoanalysis is wrongly termed "progressive" and "revolutionary," terms to which it clings as it does to its dogmas. A young person today is not likely to allow a ninety-year-old great-grandfather to tell him what is progressive; but he will accept this from his analyst in Freud's name, without realizing that the ideas he is accepting are at least ninety years old and have never been modified, given that a dogma cannot be modified. And through the influence of analysts on their patients, the effects of these dogmas are spread even beyond professional circles, preventing access to reality.

I often hear it said that we owe the discovery of child abuse to psychoanalysis. Errors like this point to the confusion reigning in this field, for in fact it is precisely psychoanalysis that has held back and continues to hold back knowledge of child abuse. I am not surprised at this confusion, for I myself failed for so long to perceive it. Although I didn't believe in dogmas, I did not notice the function they perform: that of forbidding new facts from being taken seriously and old failures from being recognized.

Among the many letters I receive that confirm this assertion, one comes from a well-known psychoanalyst who informed me that in forty years of practice he has seldom come across a victim of sexual abuse. Although some women had spoken of sexual molestations, it "transpired" in the course of psychoanalysis that these were fantasies based on infantile desires to seduce the father to perform such acts and play him off against the mother. This analyst further maintained, citing psycho-analytical authors such as Fenichel and Nunberg, that every child would enjoy sexual relations with his parents if incest were not forbidden. Guilt feelings and neuroses arise only because society prohibits this kind of relationship, thereby creating problems by this very prohibition. This letter and many others reveal with frightening clarity how far classic psychoanalysis has gone in denying reality. For, according to the American psychohistorian Lloyd de Mause, it was estimated in 1986 that more than half of American women have been sexually abused in their childhood.

In *De la honte à la colère,* Viviane Clarac tells us that at age five she was raped by her father, a high-ranking diplomat, and then was sexually abused for the next ten years. When she was twenty-five she could no longer bear to keep this secret to herself and went to a counseling clinic for rape victims. The counselor tried to explain that "incestuous relations" occur frequently and that she needn't be ashamed of her lustful feelings. Viviane's hopes of being understood were dashed, and, although she agreed to another appointment, she did not return. Why should she have? But many do return and allow themselves to go on being confused for the rest of their lives.

I don't know why this particular therapist chose phrases that totally disguise a severe case of child abuse and deceive the victim, nor do I know what personal factors were responsible for her blindness, but I do know why she cannot recognize them, and I know the source of her opinions, familiar as I am with these opinions both from my own upbringing and from my training as a psychoanalyst: The parents were never to blame. We are so strongly conditioned by this view that many of us fail to realize what it means and what the consequences are for the victim when the exertion of power and deception are described as incestuous "relations" or as imagination. No one's imagination is strong enough to visualize the horror that is inflicted on children every day in the real world. Freud has firmly locked the doors to our awareness of child abuse and has hidden the keys so carefully that ensuing generations have been unable to find them. And to this day it is rare to find a Freudian who says: "How was it possible not to see all that? For ninety years we have been listening to patients who were abused as children and we have reinforced their repression. They wanted to believe that nothing had happened to them, and their symptoms persisted. We have allied ourselves with lies!" Instead, almost all of them say the same thing as if with one voice: "Freud never disputed that sexual abuse can sometimes occur in reality as well as in imagination, but those victims rarely consult an analyst." Unfortunately they do. They come in droves, and they stay. They stay for a long time and pay heavily for the truth to remain unrecognized and the parents to be spared. They lie on the couch, four times a week, relate what comes to their minds, and wait for the miracle that never happens and in fact mustn't be allowed to happen. For the miracle would come with the truth, and it is the truth that is forbidden.

A seventy-nine-year-old woman wrote to me from the United States that for forty years she had been in analysis, with eight different analysts, for severe depression. Not until she read my books did she realize that she had been severely mistreated in her childhood. In all her analyses she had never been allowed to see this. Her analysts sought the reasons for her parents' cruel behavior in the patient's inner drives and defended the parents. The woman quoted the last sentence of my book *For Your Own Good*—"For the human soul is virtually indestructible, and its ability to rise from the ashes remains as long as the body draws breath"—and continued: "For the first time I feel really alive since I've gotten rid of those guilt feelings, since I no longer make an effort to forgive unbelievable cruelties."

The drive theory and the grave consequences arising from it are only some of the many examples of the denial of reality. Society has always shielded itself from the knowledge of child abuse. During the eighteenth century it was for a time fashionable to write autobiographies. What we can learn about childhood from these accounts is terrifying, but it is significant that they quickly went out of fashion to be replaced by psychological, sociological, and, above all, misleading and life-inimical pedagogic theories. In his fascinating book *Untertan Kind,* the pedagogue Carl-Heinz Mallet drew upon a number of pedagogic writings to demonstrate the criminal consequences of these theories. Much of what we inflict on children today could be completely avoided if our adult society— parents, doctors, teachers, social workers, and others— were better informed about the situation of the child, about the consequences of mistreatment, and above all about concrete facts.

It was a watershed in my life when I realized that psychoanalytic theories are *also* responsible for preventing the spread of this information, thus contributing to the failure to recognize child abuse.

Freud's argumentation would never have been so successful if most people had not grown up in the same tradition. His successors might soon have noticed that what looks like a reasoned argument isn't one at all. When Freud writes that it is unlikely that there are so many perverted fathers, and he therefore describes the accounts of his female patients as fantasies, that is not an argument but a childish denial of reality culminating in effect in the statement: "My papa, whom I love, is great and good and can never have done anything bad, because I couldn't imagine such a thing, because in order to live I need to believe that he loves me, protects me, doesn't abuse me, and lives up to his responsibility."

Anyone with a little insight into families with sexually abused children knows that the fathers who sexually abuse their children don't necessarily show any outward signs of being perverted. Their perversion is often restricted exclusively to their own family. Since one's own child is regarded as a chattel, most deviant, absurd, or perverted behavior by a parent toward the child can destroy the life of the child with impunity and go unnoticed. If the abused daughter does eventually arrive at a clinic suffering from schizophrenia and is treated by her psychiatrist with massive doses of medication, with the result that she will know even less than she did before, she will never find out that actually it was her father's behavior that drove her into madness. For to salvage his image, to see at least something good in her childhood, she must not know the truth. She would rather "lose" her mind.

Before publishing my first book, I gave a lecture on the mental adjustment of psychoanalysts and their presumed childhood history. After that lecture I was asked: "But you can't seriously mean that all psychoanalysts were abused children?" I replied: "I can't be sure, I can only assume it. But I would say that no one can be a psychoanalyst who has experienced abuse—widespread as it is—in his own childhood and no longer needs to deny it. For in that case psychoanalytic theories cease to make sense."

Later I found my assumption reinforced when I learned that some analysts have no recollection whatsoever of the first seventeen years of their lives and see nothing strange in that. The result is that, with such a massive repression of his own childhood and puberty, a person will do anything, *must* do anything, to prevent being reminded by his patients of his own suffering. Freud provided the necessary means for that procedure, and analysts in their extremity reach for such means as an addict reaches for his drug. They pay for this drug with their blindness.

A woman journalist told me that a retired psychiatrist, formerly in charge of a large clinic, said to her: "You needn't get so worked up about child abuse; what you call abuse is something the child can survive without any great difficulty. Children are experts in survival." In this statement the doctor was doubtless correct, but the tragedy is that he obviously didn't know the price of this survival, any more than he knew that he had also paid the price himself and had made others pay. For forty years he had treated female and male patients, prescribed medication for them, talked encouragingly to them, and never once grasped that the grave psychotic conditions he was observing every day were nothing but attempts to describe, in the language of symptoms, the mistreatments and confusion of their childhood.

Dr. Elisabeth Trube-Becker, a specialist in forensic

medicine, maintains that, based on the most recent studies, for every reported case of sexual abuse of children there are fifty unreported cases to be assumed. If we add the physical and psychic abuses not primarily sexual, we arrive at the unavoidable conclusion *that crimes against children represent the most frequent of all types of crime.* A further conclusion leads us inescapably to the shocking realization that millions of experts (doctors, lawyers, psychologists, psychiatrists, and social workers) deal with the consequences of these crimes without being aware of, or being allowed to say—because of their own blindness and self-censoring—what is involved.

When I look at these conditions of child abuse with open eyes I am glad that I am not doomed by a curse to be turned into a pillar of salt but that as a person of the modern age I have the opportunity of repeatedly drawing attention to these pernicious and destructive facts—and even to cause other people to be increasingly alert.

Elisabeth Trube-Becker seems also to have grasped this opportunity. She doesn't hesitate to call a spade a spade and publicly air the facts with which she is confronted every day, nor does she resort to abstruse theories or palatable ideologies designed to provide a shield from the truth and obscure the facts. She writes:

The estimated number of unreported cases of sexual abuse of children is far greater than that of other forms of maltreatment. For each reported case of sexual child abuse there are twenty cases that never come to light. In terms of offenses committed within the immediate family, the ratio is said to be as high as 1:50.

Even technical literature contains few, if any, reports on sexual offenses against children, and in any that do appear the incident is regarded as rare and the child as the seducer. Reference is made to the sexuality and fantasy of the child, as well as to Freud and the so-called Oedipus complex, on which researchers have most recently, and justifiably, been casting doubt.

It is claimed that the child is lying, although a child in prepuberty—the most frequent victim of sexual assault—virtually never lies, if only because he is in no position to concoct something in his imagination that he has never experienced.

True, even a child is not an asexual creature. He has sensations and impulses. He is curious. He desires and needs affection, skin contact, and tenderness. A child's natural desire for human warmth and attention, even for material advantages, must not be exploited by adults in any way for sexual acts. The responsibility for what happens lies always with the adult and not with the child, as was actually claimed in a judgment of the *Landesgericht* in Kempten, West Germany, as recently as July 1984. The judge made allowances for the defendant inasmuch as the initiative for the act "had to a certain extent been taken by his precocious victim"—a seven-year-old girl!

But why do so many of these criminal acts remain in obscurity?

Why is the sexual abuse of children still regarded as an extremely rare occurrence hardly worth mentioning?

The reasons are manifold.

1. Often the victim is a toddler, or the sexual abuse begins at the baby or toddler stage, at a time when the child is not yet able to articulate.

When fathers fondle their children's genitals, or mothers misuse a baby for pornographic photos (my own case), this represents the onset of increasing sexual violence that can extend undiscovered over many years. No one endowed with a reasonable amount of common sense will proceed on the assumption that poking a finger into the vagina of a six-month-old baby girl, to see "whether she's ready for it" (as shown in the series "Sexuality Today"), constitutes an isolated occurrence.

2. The older child shrinks from speaking up, especially when the father is the perpetrator. The father's authority and threats prevent the child, in his search for help, from confiding in others. And to whom should the child turn when the person who is looked to for protection so criminally abuses that trust?

3. If the child does succeed in unburdening herself—ninety percent of the victims are girls—she is dismissed as a liar and regarded as the guilty party (which is how she feels) or even accused of being a "little whore." She is urged by other family members to withdraw her accusations, or else the family will be ruined and lose its provider.

It is rare under these circumstances for a sexually abused child to summon the psychic strength to tell what happened, especially since a hatred develops in many children for their own body, which is "to blame" for it all.

"It was my body's fault that this was happening to me. Without it Daddy wouldn't be able to touch me."

Even workers in youth welfare offices, inexperienced in problems of this kind, tend to respond to such reports with: "The child herself is probably to blame."

4. The attitude of the mother, who is worried about losing the family provider or is afraid of her husband, also figures in bringing the offense to light, especially since she often occupies an inferior position in the family—or also because she has no inkling of what is going on in her absence.

5. If a doctor is consulted, he is not likely to include the consequences of sexual abuse among his diagnostic alternatives. Doctors show themselves to be totally unsuspecting and disbelieving toward sexual abuse of children, nor do they recognize behavioral disturbances as a result of sexual abuse.

Psychologists and psychotherapists will first of all banish the child's report to the realm of fantasy, as Freud did: "Freud shrank from reality."

67

6. The general indifference toward the weaker person, but also the helplessness of adults who don't know how they should behave, are further factors preventing the uncovering of the crime.

Men have problems discussing the sexual abuse of children, for fear of being regarded as presumptive perpetrators, a fear I have sensed in various discussions.

The subject being addressed is immediately "blocked off." Men find it distasteful even to think of including the sexual abuse of children within the realm of possibilities.

7. When a case is brought to court, the impression is often given that incest is a very rare occurrence.

It is amazing with how much discretion the perpetrator continues to be treated, whereas hardly a thought is given to the child as victim. The child is subjected to every possible examination and eventually presented as lacking in credibility. There is even a tendency to exonerate the father especially and to incriminate the child, in order to trivialize the offense.

8. The deed must appear to have taken place without violence—no perpetrator and no victim. In fact, the large proportion of children who undergo pedosexual acts is actually cited to demonstrate that this is quite a common occurrence, and that harmful consequences can normally not be observed. (Because, in my opinion, no one cares about them.)

It may be true that only in very rare cases is there physical evidence of sexual as distinct from physical abuse. Behavioral disturbances, on the other hand, which may be of greater or lesser severity and may be detrimental to future life, show that sexual abuse, especially when committed by the father, cannot be experienced without consequences.

Doctors as well as specialists in forensic medicine are consulted in cases of sexual child abuse only when there are injuries to the genital organs; in the case of pregnancy (today often terminated); when venereal diseases or other evidence of abuse are present; or if the child dies.

9. In the opinion of some German authors and many psychotherapists, the behavior of young girls—although surely not applicable to babies and toddlers unless they are to be blamed for their plump thighs or kicking their legs when their diapers are being changed—can often provoke the offense. It is claimed, among other things, that child victims of sex offenses have an exceptionally strong interest in sex and are often charming, attractive, and seductive.

The poor perpetrator! In the light of this, how can any personal blame be ascribed to him?

All I can say is that the behavior of young girls who experiment a bit with their seductive arts within the security of their own family is entirely normal and does not justify either incest or sexual abuse by strangers; and it certainly does not represent an invitation to adults to perform sexual acts, which as a rule are instigated not by the child but by the male adult, who alone bears the responsibility.

The child's natural desire for tenderness, human warmth, and attention, for cuddling or even material advantages, must never be abused by adults for sexual acts. In spite of this, the blame for the occurrence is sought, and, of course, also found, not in the perpetrator but invariably in the child, or even in the mother.

It is the psychologists especially who attempt to reverse the perpetrator/victim relationship, i.e., to present the perpetrator as the victim of the child's seduction, a shift of responsibility—responsibility which, I must emphasize again, invariably rests with the adult.

10. Finally it is claimed that government institutions have no right to invade the privacy of the family. The family is taboo. It must be preserved under any circumstances, even at the expense of the child. The best place for the child, it is claimed, is still within the security of the family. This is acceptable, provided the family genuinely protects the child, and the child can develop freely and can unconditionally trust the

other members of the family, and provided his right to physical and psychic integrity is acknowledged by the whole family; it is not acceptable, however, when the power of the adult is exerted improperly and the child is forced to satisfy the sexual needs of parents or other persons.

Of all forms of sexual abuse of children, incest is the most frequent, representing the largest estimated number of unreported cases, as a result of, among other things, the commandment to remain silent, the denial of the deed, as well as the silence on the part of the rest of the family. . . .

On the basis of a few individual cases, the erroneous impression has arisen, especially among psychologists, that incest is very rare, occurring only in socioeconomically deprived circles, in a lower-class milieu, in conjunction with violence, alcoholism, unemployment, etc.

From a forensic-medical point of view, this is not acceptable. Incest occurs at all social levels, regardless of religion or ethnic background, but never shows up in any crime statistics. In the first year of life the victims are children of both sexes. . . .

According to Baurmann, ninety percent of rape victims are young girls or women, two thirds of them between the ages of five and thirteen. . . .

According to Kempe, incest cases have increased considerably in the United States, which is also true of Europe. Nowadays, however, these cases are more likely to become known and brought into the open. People are beginning to be concerned, and "the daughters no longer remain silent" (Miller 1983). Cases of incest can extend over many years and become known only when the father opposes the daughter's wish to leave the parental home, and beats, throttles, or even kills her.

As she grows up, the daughter usually manages to form ties outside the family, to make friends and confide in them, provided she still has a sufficient sense of self-worth to take active steps. Confirmed in her resolve, she then finds the courage to leave the parental home, and this inevitably puts an end to the incestuous relationship between father and daughter. The abuse is never mentioned again, never shows up in any statistics, and, needless to say, can never be prosecuted.

Sometimes, after leaving her parents' home, the girl plucks up enough courage to speak about the years of abuse, to break the imposed silence, and even to lay charges.

But the desire for separation may also have fatal consequences, as can resistance to abuse: a brother kills his sixteen-year-old sister because she resists, he violates her dead body, then strangles his ten-year-old brother because he has been a witness.

It was not only in ancient times that the child spent his first years in an atmosphere of sexual abuse; this happened well into the nineteenth century. Kissing and sucking the baby's breast, touching the testicles, the nipples, and the genital organs, licking the skin with the tongue, anal intercourse with boys, the sale of children to child bordellos, and much else that is scarcely imaginable, were taken for granted—pedophilic manipulations that we should not try to encourage by abolishing any penal laws against them.

Furthermore, bordellos exist today, not only in Asian countries, where little girls are systematically subjected to sexual exploitation and abuse. In Thailand, girls are kept prisoner in bordellos and, with beatings and stimulants, forced into prostitution. According to the statements of seven little girls who survived a fire in a bordello on January 30, 1984, they were kept like slaves. The children were never allowed to leave the building and were chained to each other when one tried to escape. One child told a doctor in the hospital that, ever since she had been abducted from her village two years earlier, she had been forced to engage in sexual intercourse every night from six p.m. until five a.m. with at least twelve men.

Most of the bordello customers are tourists from Europe, including West Germany, who satisfy their sexual urges by availing themselves of children forced into prostitution. In

71

Hong Kong there are even five-year-old prostitutes. What kind of men are they who resort to children to satisfy their sexual urges?

Child prostitution is also a problem in the industrial countries. UNICEF has estimated that some two million children of both sexes are being sexually exploited throughout the world. This does not take into account the sexual abuse that occurs within the family.

Elisabeth Trube-Becker has enumerated the serious consequences of mistreatment suffered in childhood and has cited some shocking examples. To her list should be added the victim's compulsion to repeat those repressed experiences on the defenseless young if no enlightened witness is available to help him rid himself of the repression.

In the therapy I personally underwent, I discovered that, with every inner confrontation with my parents, the guilt feelings that had been instilled in me reinforced my repression, barred my access to reality, and blocked my experiencing of pain. It was only when I could query my supposed guilt that those feelings surfaced. And only when I could feel that, *without* any guilt on my part, I had been ignored, not taken seriously, scarcely even noticed by my parents, did I realize what had happened. It became clear that it had not been up to me to teach my parents a sense of responsibility, that it had not been in my power as a babe in arms to render them capable of loving. The only thing I had been able to do was show them that I was useful, that I could be exploited, and that I would never respond with reproaches. At the time, life offered me no other option.

As soon as I had become aware of the blocking function of those guilt feelings, I noticed that they always occurred and disturbed my sleep when a fragment of some traumatic memory emerged. The next day I would want to negate everything I had discovered for myself the day before. I either forgot my newfound knowledge, or felt compelled to deny it, or was miserable because I had been capable of such appalling thoughts about my parents. Here again the same inevitable sequence was at work that had compelled Freud to betray his discovery.

Many therapists often observe this resistance in their patients and mistakenly interpret it as proof that reality does, after all, elude our grasp. And eventually the patient himself is uncertain whether he was describing actual memories or mere fantasies. The child's inner struggle for the image of the good father or the good mother can be so intense that not only the patient but everyone around him succumbs to the confusion. Freud's view that it is possible to invent something worse than the reality experienced did a great deal of harm in my own case, too. How I longed to believe that all signals were deceiving me, that things weren't really that bad, and that only my suspicion was wicked and unfair. How I wished that psychoanalysis might be right, because of my longing to cling to the illusion of loving parents.

As time went on it became clear to me that the idea of children inventing traumas is absurd. Anyone is free to check on the natural law that human beings will avoid pain rather than seek it. They seek pleasure, joy, reassurance. Masochism is no exception to this rule: It is a compulsion to inflict new suffering on oneself to keep former suffering repressed. The masochist who at great expense has himself whipped by a prostitute and insists on sitting on a chamber pot during the procedure is obeying a compulsion to reproduce the trauma of his toilet training and to keep the memory repressed at all costs. Another law of life is that the idealization of the parents with the aid of fantasy and repression helps the child to survive; thus to attribute bad things to one's nearest and dearest would run counter to natural defenses and the law of life. It follows that a child *will never invent traumas.* On the contrary, to survive the child must resort to fantasy to make the pain bearable.

Thus, for example, sexually mistreated children often claim to have killed a baby, but because their stories cannot be substantiated they are called liars. If they come to court, all their statements can then be deemed invalid. It never occurs to the judges that these children are experiencing their mistreatment as a murder of the baby each of them had once been and that they are describing their own inner situation. The fantasy of the murdered baby is a way of expressing what really happened—a way that serves to mitigate the actual trauma. For it is easier to see oneself as a criminal than to know and feel that one was, and is, an innocent victim who must be prepared at all times for torture and persecution. Every patient clings to fantasies in which he sees himself in the active role so as to escape the pain of being defenseless and helpless. To achieve this he will accept guilt feelings, although they bind him to neurosis.

The remembered and documented facts often reveal only a small part of the fate a child has had to suffer. The larger part consists of the repressed experiences that cannot be told because they were never consciously experienced. And with therapists who shrink from the reality of child abuse, they will never be found. For a therapist to assert, "I always believe my patients," doesn't mean that he can't still fail to perceive their repression and denial. He cannot, of course, know more about his patient's concrete past than the patient is capable of finding out himself. The patient must uncover the facts with the aid of his feelings; he must examine his discoveries, query his own statements, until he arrives at the certainty: Such and such actually happened. But the realm of the possible is infinite, and *that* is what the therapist must know. There is nothing that could not be inflicted on a child. This knowledge enables the therapist to accompany the patient on his journey, a journey that often leads through hells and torture chambers. These must be returned to, again and again, until every detail of the traumatic scene can be experienced, to allow the effect of the trauma to dissolve and the injury at last to heal.

Yet most of the therapists whom I knew as I searched for answers in my own life were totally ignorant of the existence of these torture chambers. They contented themselves with admitting that every childhood encompasses some difficult moments: separation from the parents, for instance, or the birth of younger siblings, or some other "unavoidable frustrations." When they can no longer classify the parents' behavior as unavoidable frustration, they speak of a "latent psychosis" in the mother or father, thus once again circumventing the problem of actual child abuse. It may very well be a case of psychotic behavior on the part of the parents, but the important thing to know is that such behavior continues to be ignored by society as long as it is visited on one's own children. This knowledge is imperative if one is truly to accompany and understand the patient, especially at those moments when he fights tooth and nail against the truth because it is so inconceivable, so at odds with life.

But if one knows that virtually the only way a child was able to survive his childhood tortures was through repression, it will be possible to give the patient the support he needs to rid himself of his repression.

In discussions about the sexual abuse of children, the question constantly comes up: Why does the girl's mother ignore the signals, or why, through her attitude, does she make it impossible for her daughter to confide in her? The mother's behavior is particularly hard to understand when it turns out that she herself was abused as a child. Yet the key to understanding lies in this information. It is those very mothers who suffered similar abuse in their childhood, and have kept it repressed ever since, who are blind and deaf to the situation of their daughters. They cannot bear to be reminded of their own history, and so they fail the child.

Unfortunately it is at this point that the feminist movement, which has done so much to make the public finally aware of child abuse, comes up against its ideological limits. It sees the problem as being rooted exclusively in the patriarchy, in the male exertion of power. This simplification leaves many questions unasked. Perhaps it is too early to ask these questions since they would threaten the image of the idealized mother. Yet we must wonder: What causes a man to rape women and children? Who made him so evil? In my experience it is not always the fathers alone. We would also have to wonder what options there are for a humiliated woman *not* to abuse her small child for her own needs; even in cultures in which a woman counts for nothing, society invests her with unlimited power over her young child. The further question arises of how much responsibility an adult woman will assume for her child if as a little girl she was abused by her father and what she will inflict on her son if she keeps that former occurrence repressed.

I have noticed that some feminists don't care to listen to such questions, yet they are at a loss when they constantly hear of mothers who, instead of protecting their sexually abused daughters, leave them to their fate or even punish them. The simple explanation given is that of fear of the husband. These feminists are reluctant to accept the fact that a woman who has had a sheltered childhood and a protective mother is not likely to marry a man whom she fears and who will abuse her child because she was not made blind; she was not forced to love what did not deserve to be loved. Her sensors would warn her of an abusive man and she would not marry him.

These considerations are not intended to detract from the merits of the feminist movement in its approach to child abuse but rather to encourage the breaking down of old boundaries. The process of exposing lies must not be brought to a standstill by new ideological untruths, by illusions and idealizations. The situation of an adult woman confronted by a brutal man is not the same as that of a small child. Although, because of her childhood, the woman can see herself as equally helpless and thus may overlook her chances of defense, she is in fact no longer helpless. Even when her rights are inadequate, even when the courts are on the side of the man, an adult woman can speak up, report, look for allies, and she can scream (assuming she hasn't, as a child, learned not to). But above all she need no longer repress the past, she can suffer pain and insults without new injuries arising from them. It is only in the child that traumas are bound to lead to psychic wounds because they damage the organism in its growth process. These injuries can heal if one dares to see them, or they can remain unhealed if one is forced to go on ignoring them. In Chapter 6 I use the example of a family to illustrate these thoughts in detail.

The feminist movement will forfeit none of its strength if it finally admits that mothers also abuse their children. Only the truth, even the most uncomfortable, endows a movement with the strength to change society, not the denial of the truth. When men abuse their women and the women put up with it, both the violence of the men and the tolerance of the women are consequences of early child abuse. Hence young children, male as well as female, can become victims of adults of *either* sex. When sensitive, nonbrutal women (and men) are incapable of protecting their children from the brutality of their partner, one must attribute this inability to the blinding process and the intimidation experienced in their own childhood. That is the simple truth. Only when these roots of all violence are exposed is it possible to examine the phenomena without retouching or embellishing them.

When a female therapist has been taught that men are solely to blame for all the evil in the world, she will, of course, be able to support her female patients when they eventually discover that they have been sexually abused by their fathers, grandfathers, or brothers: Unlike the followers of the drive theory, she will not talk them out of this truth. But as long as the truth about the mother who allowed the abuse to happen, who failed to protect the child and ignored her distress, is kept out of sight, the full reality is not allowed to be either perceived or acknowledged. And as long as the child's feelings cannot be experienced, the rage against men—a rage she can already experience—remains impotent; it can even remain coupled with the undissolved loyalty and devotion toward the father or other abusive men.

When mothers are defended as pathetic victims, the female patient will not discover that with a loving, protective, perceptive, and courageous mother she could never have been abused by her father or brother. A daughter who has learned from her mother that she is worth protecting will find protection among strangers too and will be able to defend herself. When she has learned what love is, she will not succumb to simulated love. But a child who was merely pushed aside and disciplined, who never experienced soothing caresses, is not aware that anything like nonexploitative caresses can exist. She has no choice but to accept any closeness she is offered rather than be destroyed. Under certain circumstances she will even accept sexual abuse for the sake of finding at least some affection rather than freezing up entirely. When, as an adult woman, she comes to realize that she was cheated out of love, she may be ashamed of her former need and hence feel guilty. She will blame herself because she dare not blame her mother, who failed to satisfy the child's need or perhaps even condemned it.

Psychoanalysts protect the father and embroider the sexual abuse of the child with the Oedipus, or Electra, complex, while some feminist therapists idealize the mother, thus hindering access to the child's first traumatic experiences with the mother. Both approaches can lead to a dead end, since the dissolving of pain and fear is not possible until the full truth of the facts can be seen and accepted.

But even in the absence of ideological motives, the

truth can be disregarded in therapies if the patient is offered no tools to deal with his feelings and to systematically query and test his hypotheses. Even the harshest reproaches directed at the parents won't help the patient achieve liberation as long as the truth remains inaccessible. This will be the case if, for example, the child had a father in whose presence he could scarcely utter a word without being interrupted and barked at. This patient may for a very long time find it impossible to achieve an inner confrontation with his father and to articulate his accusations. The liberated feelings are directed first against the mother, who terrorized the child less. The reverse may also happen—that the child feared his father less than he feared his mother and that the patient first accuses his father, quite unconsciously because the earlier experiences are still inaccessible, of things he actually experienced with his mother. Thus, based on self-protection and fear, a distorted picture of the past takes shape. In the course of therapy these distortions can be corrected, provided the therapy is aimed at discovering the reality. If it is, the therapist knows that the patient can accuse only the parent in whom he still had a modicum of confidence and not the parent in whose presence he had been paralyzed with fear. The therapist will help him discover the truth of his history so that he *doesn't blame the wrong people* but blames only those who really deserve it and, moreover, only for those deeds *that were actually committed.* For nobody achieves freedom by blaming people who in reality never harmed him. By directing diffuse, nonspecific, and unsubstantiated accusations at surrogate persons, the patient will achieve no improvement of his condition but will often remain in a state of disastrous confusion. Liberation comes with the ability to defend oneself where it is necessary and appropriate. The more realistic a person becomes and the more he frees himself of ideological and theoretical trimmings, the better he will succeed.

FIVE

PRETENDING TO WANT TO KNOW

A JOURNALIST who was very familiar with my books wanted to produce a television program dealing with the causes and consequences of child abuse. Although she was a highly regarded member of her team and had already created several programs on a number of subjects, her plan met with intense resistance on the part of everyone concerned. All the same she did not give up the idea and after several months achieved her object: She was allowed to film conversations with those involved (parents and children) but was allocated only five minutes of broadcast time per conversation. These five-minute interviews were then integrated into four one-hour programs on which a number of diverse problems were discussed that had nothing to do with the subject of child abuse. The programs were interspersed with popular songs, interviews with singers, demonstrations of the latest electronic discoveries, and more of a similar nature. But at the same time a telephone number was also flashed on the screen for viewers to dial if they had a problem concerning child abuse. A psychiatrist and a psychoanalyst were present in the studio to answer their questions. This offer was taken up by a great many viewers; the telephone was busier than with any previous subject. The psychoanalyst said, among other things, that there was no reason to have guilt feelings if one smacked one's child; one could phone a therapist and discuss these "problems." What he didn't say was that such discussions of "problems" usually led nowhere. Perhaps he didn't know this, or did not know it yet.

In the fourth and last of these programs, the journalist tried to broach the subject of the consequences of child abuse for our future. What kind of people, she asked, will these babies grow up into, these babies whom today we prevent from crying by giving them tranquilizers, thus deadening their feelings? Almost in midsentence she was interrupted by the moderator, who, with his masklike smile, did his utmost to reassure parents that everything being shown and discussed on the program wasn't really that bad, and, if it was, there were so many phone numbers to call. Sidestepping any show of concern, he had already delegated his responsibility to the phone number and diverted the audience with constant new spectacles best designed to silence their own concern.

Did those involved in the television program really have a desire to know how to avoid abuses, or was it a matter of not wanting to know? Why is so much done ostensibly to inform the public, while at the same time so much effort is directed at preventing the spread of this information by diverting the public's attention and emotions with other subjects, thus making it impossible for them to benefit from what little information they are given? The answer is always the same: The organizers of this program also had a childhood and also have parents. Were they to provide complete information to their audience along with a chance to absorb it, their own repressions might be badly shaken. That would produce great anxiety. Is it possible to tell the organizers of the program that they were afraid of this topic? They would in any event dispute this since they, of course, aren't aware of any fear. If they were able to feel this fear, they wouldn't have to provide so much diversion. But people whose feelings were deadened in childhood know nothing of their own fear. They don't realize the lengths to which they go to avoid the feeling of fear. However, when they work in the media everything they do can have a powerful positive or negative effect—on themselves and above all on others.

It is this same repressed (unconscious) fear that causes gynecologists and midwives to make such a business of delivering a baby. The infant is weighed, measured, injected, as if its very survival depended on all these activities: In fact, this is often claimed to be so. That it is not so was demonstrated some fifteen years ago by the French physician Frederick Leboyer with his films and books. The newborn child who has come naturally into the world, without destructive intervention, doesn't cry but lies contentedly, even smiling, on the mother's stomach. The point is that the baby is not treated like a slab of wood, not measured, bathed, and weighed under a glaring light and assailed by loud noises. Instead, his feelings and the shock he has undergone are taken into account, and the baby is treated like an extremely fragile human being.

The scientific value of the Leboyer films should have radically altered our child-delivery practices, but we are still a long way from that. In fact, after a period of awareness of and concern for the natural process of birth in the 1970s, the technologizing of the delivery room is actually increasing at an alarming rate. The psychic sufferings of the newborn and the consequences of the repression of those sufferings seem to remain hidden to the experts, with few exceptions. Leboyer's discovery is said to be unscientific, even dangerous, and in most hospitals normal births resemble operations on sick patients. The inducing of labor is becoming more and more common in many countries, with the result that a large proportion of newborns must first be treated in the intensive care unit. This means, of course, separation from the mother.

As a result, a crucial opportunity for mother and child is missed, for it is in those first few minutes and hours after birth that the presence of the infant arouses and encourages the mother's caring capacity, so essential for her bonding with the child. A mother in labor who as a baby experienced a great deal of affection will immediately rebel against cruel hospital regulations. But women who were left alone at the time of their own birth and who received no physical warmth will accept hospital regulations without protest, regarding them as the most normal thing in the world. Sometimes they react to the separation from their newborn infant with depression or physical complaints, causing doctors and nurses to direct their attention at treating those ailments. Rarely if ever are the mothers told that those ailments are warding off the new and the old pain of separation. Far more often they are told that postpartum depression is a "perfectly normal" manifestation that can easily be taken care of with medication.

That which occurs often is erroneously described by many doctors as "normal." No doubt it is true that the mothers of today who were born in the bleak, sterile hospitals of the fifties and sixties are not likely to have had good childbirth experiences. But this shared fate is far from normal or inevitable, based as it is on cultural rather than biological factors. Recent, more humane innovations prove this unequivocally.

A woman told me that she accepted the postpartum separation from her first child without demur, although she was not fully aware of how desperate she felt. She merely suffered from her depression and from inflamed breasts—all the more reason for the hospital staff to keep her separated from her baby. When her second child was born, she found the hospital staff more sympathetic and understanding, and the baby was placed on her stomach immediately after birth. Her utter delight over this close and blissful sharing enabled her for the first time to feel the old pain of her loneliness as a baby. Moreover, she found that in the ensuing years her relationship with this second child was much less "burdensome" and surprisingly carefree.

I have also heard of similar experiences and their influences on later relationships from other mothers who were lucky enough, thanks to a good childbirth experience, to become aware of old wounds and allow them to heal. These women will no longer be impressed by the wonders of technology and pharmacology. Animal experiments have also shown that animals whose young were taken from them immediately after birth subsequently showed no interest in their own young or those of others. It is no coincidence that the experiences of mothers and recent studies have attracted little attention among most doctors, in fact have fallen on deaf ears, since the technologizing of obstetrics serves to fend off fear among those present. The fear thus repulsed by the doctors relates to the once repressed pain of their own birth and to the possible resurgence of their own memories. It blocks their ability to use new insights for practical purposes and thoughtlessly sacrifices the happiness of future human beings. And all this is served up to the intimidated mother as progress.

The gynecologists, who know scarcely anything of their own fear, justify their bustling activity with concern for the well-being of the newborn infant. The television people justify their diversionary programming with the requirements of the visual medium and the alleged impatience of the viewer, who is said to demand pictures and spectacles and to be unable to concentrate for long on the spoken word. That claim, repeated over and over again, is manifestly untrue, especially when the topic is child abuse, which concerns every individual. This is borne out by the reactions that invariably ensue when the media genuinely explore the topic. A Norwegian journalist once interviewed me for almost two hours and allowed me to develop my ideas without ever interrupting me. After the broadcast she received many telephone calls from people who thanked her not only for the information but also for the way in which she had listened without interfering. Yet the old so-called tried-and-true formats guarantee that the commandment "Thou shalt not be aware" will be followed in television and in radio and the press as well.

A New York monthly, for example, described to me by my American publisher as "serious and strictly scientific," wanted to publish an interview with me. It was to be conducted by a psychotherapist who, I was told, had studied my books at length. After receiving assurance that nothing would be changed without my consent, I accepted. But the drama began after the actual interview had taken place.

For a whole year the art department of this scientific periodical maintained that the interview could not possibly be published unless I allowed the staff photographer to take pictures of me. I consistently rejected this demand because I refuse to give anyone the copyright to my photographs, and I finally suggested that the plan to publish the interview be abandoned. Only then did the editors let themselves be persuaded to accept a photograph that I supplied. This deviation from their "sacred" principles was due to the efforts of the editor who had carefully worked on the text and for whom it was important to have it finally published. She kept her promise and consulted me over every suggested change.

Three months after publication of the authorized interview in this scientific journal, the German edition of a magazine whose scope of interests has nothing whatever to do with my ideas published a German version of the original English-language interview cut down to one third and grossly distorted. The publisher went so far as to claim that I had granted the "interview" to the German magazine. As it later turned out, one and the same publishing house controls both journals, which made the "transfer" possible in the first place.

Although it may seem obvious that solely financial interests were behind this duping of the reader, my experience with the subject of child abuse has taught me that such unforeseen switches and conflicting activities in the media do not always have such a simple explanation. They also occur where there are no obvious vested interests, let alone financial sacrifices. At times one gains the impression that for many people the topic of "childhood" is enough to automatically evoke derision, arrogance, meanness, or even illegal acts—precisely the same attitudes and behavior they themselves experienced and learned in their childhood from adults.

What actually happened in the case of my interview? A psychotherapist travels from New York to Europe to obtain information from me that seems important to her and that obviously disturbs her. The editor later reacts in a similar way when she edits the text. I see no reason to refuse the journal permission to publish, for the precision of my statements seems to me to be guaranteed, and that's all that counts for me: the intactness of my ideas. But in the end the very opposite of what I expect happens: With the German edition the journal breaks its promise, given to me in writing, that nothing will be changed, cut, or added without my consent. It allows my text to be arbitrarily cut by unauthorized persons without reference to myself. It allows a faulty translation from English into German to be published without asking me to authorize the text. Further, it allows this whole farce to appear in a completely distorting frame. Thus the work intended to enlighten the public on the exploitation of children and their repression—a work per-

89

formed by three people with the expenditure of much care and time—is with a single blow rendered ineffective. It is as if one hand brings something up into the light and the other hand instantly thrusts it back into the darkness.

That this phenomenon is not an isolated case is illustrated by the following example.

Since many senior editors have been on the receiving end of "poisonous pedagogy" to the fullest extent, and defend it, they block important information that might cause them fear. They also prevent younger female and male journalists from passing on new insights that the younger people, perhaps thanks to a somewhat more relaxed upbringing, are already able to accept. Thus the commandments of "poisonous pedagogy" are perpetuated unnoticed in our society, and information that might save humanity from self-destruction is sabotaged. I will describe here the experience I had with one journal because this story clearly illustrates the kind of resistance I meet in trying to present the situation of the child and obtain a hearing for his voice.

In the summer of 1986 I wrote a preface for a new British edition of my book *The Drama of the Gifted Child*. My publisher offered an advance copy of my preface to a German magazine. The German editor found the text too theoretical for her readers, but she cordially invited me to write an article for her magazine. In it I was to address her readers directly and explain to parents why they find it so difficult to control their anger against their children; parents should be shown a way out of their vicious circle, the editor felt. The article was to avoid theoretical terms and get as close as possible to the parents' situation.

That letter and its reasoning made sense to me, so I

wrote an article for the magazine that has been reprinted in the appendix to this book. Although I did not expect any journal in Germany to be prepared to publish this text, I could not write it any differently. Since the editor told me over the phone that I needn't be so pessimistic and that her team was very open to new insights, I had reason to hope. Her first reaction to my article seemed to confirm my hope. She wrote: "So far I have only been able to glance through the manuscript, but my first impression is: This is exactly what I had in mind."

Her reaction pleased me very much. I was already inclined to think that the fears of my generation must have blinded me to the increasing openness of younger people. But I was soon to find out differently.

After a few weeks I learned that the deputy editor-in-chief found the text interesting and had taken it home for a more thorough reading but had meanwhile become ill. On eventually recovering and returning to his office, he expressed the opinion—so I was told—that there was no objection whatever to the content and that the article was important, but too long: It would have to be cut by a few pages. And above all the part about Hitler would have to come out because readers wouldn't understand my thoughts in the proposed abbreviated form.

This opinion seemed to me somewhat contradictory. A journal aimed chiefly at informing parents about parenthood receives an article that the editors consider important and correct, an article of the precise length initially agreed on, yet those responsible feel obliged to shorten it. On the other hand, they say that the reference to Hitler, a reference that might be very helpful in understanding the rest, must be taken out because it was too global and required explanation. Why wasn't I requested to give this explanation?

I asked the original editor whether the judgment "too long" didn't in fact mean: This truth is unbearable, we cannot publish it in such a simple, unequivocal and undisguised form. She assured me I was mistaken and promised that she would soon let me have her suggested shortened version.

She kept her word. The result was courageous, honest, without embellishment, without distortion. This young woman, herself the mother of two small children, seemed to have been able to bear the truth. She told me it might be a shock for some, but a wholesome one, and the matter was too important not to be published. We are no longer living in Sigmund Freud's times, I thought: Things are beginning to change after all.

But I rejoiced too soon. Two weeks after I called the editor and congratulated her on her courage and her brilliant condensing, I received a letter from her telling me that the editor-in-chief had now read the text himself and judged it to be too difficult for their readers to understand. So the publication of this article was stopped. I was invited to give an interview a few months later for this journal: There were plans for an issue on child abuse, and my views on the subject of "punishment" could, together with the views of others, be put up for discussion.

I was very disappointed that my efforts to inform parents about their situation and thus spare them further guilt could not be supported by the very journal that purports to want to help parents. When, five years ago, similar problems arose with the German women's magazine *Brigitte,* I did at least experience something positive from that quarter. It is owing to the courage of the editors at that time that the great plight of incest victims in Germany finally came to the attention of the public.

My experience with one journal as I have described it is actually no longer typical. I have noticed that the journalists who interview me now show much greater understanding of the situation of the child than they did even seven years ago. It does, of course, happen that an interview in which I was perfectly well understood is ultimately not allowed to appear because it is "too long" or "too short" or for some other strange reasons that never —as is always emphasized—have anything to do with the content. I am under the impression that the journalists in question seem to believe this reasoning themselves, or perhaps think they have to believe it—not only because their job depends on the goodwill of their superiors but also because many superiors speak the language of their own parents, a language that renders a person more powerless than he really is because it touches old wounds and thus reactivates the defenselessness of the child.

Fear of the truth can also be illustrated by the actions of the courts, whose specific task it surely should be to discover the truth. In all countries I know, many of those accused of sexual child abuse are released from detention because of "lack of proof." They even proceed to file countersuits claiming damages, maintaining that their professional careers have been destroyed by the allegations (and not by the crimes committed). Many of the victims withdraw their charges because they are accused again and again of having invented all the stories. In France, Great Britain, Germany, and so many other countries, the judges seldom believe children and require "proofs." However, anybody should know today that only in a very small percentage of cases can sexual abuse be "proved" if judges don't believe children's reports.

There is nothing easier to silence than the true voice of the child, especially in a courtroom. Most judges don't seem to know this, and they allow the victims to be questioned like adult witnesses. A therapist who was treating one such six-year-old "witness" once wrote to me describing what can result from such interrogation. His patient, a little girl, grew panicky during the questioning and, when she was required to sit on the big chair and couldn't touch the floor with her feet, her unease rose to such a pitch that she was prepared to recant all her former statements just so she could feel the ground under her feet again and escape.

At first sight it is amazing that judges—women as well as men—should know so little about the soul of the child. Weren't they once children? Yes, children with their own history of repression. They seem to be blind to a very crucial factor: the fact that the well-paid and eloquent defense attorneys eliminate the voice of truth from the courtroom, even before the court pronounces judgment, by resorting to psychic terrorizing and brainwashing, so that the truth ultimately remains undiscoverable. Attorneys disseminate the *impression* that they are concerned with truth and justice, but neither of these is to be found with closed eyes. It should be the duty of judges to find a way out of the monster labyrinth each case of sexual abuse brings to light. Instead, they act just as they learned to do as children. They serve the interests of the adults—of the often unscrupulous attorneys and of the perpetrators—and betray the child and thus also the truth. If they listen to the children with attentive ears and look at their faces with alert eyes, what kind of memories would surface within them? They prefer to shield themselves from those memories by resorting to courtroom routine and by delivering up already grossly mistreated children to new, cruel mistreatment, sacrificing them to the ignorance of the adults. This they do without batting an eye and without the slightest twinge of conscience because they themselves once, as children, were sacrificed to the same ignorance and have never been allowed to perceive this.

SIX

THE HIGH COST
OF LYING

WHY IS IT SO DIFFICULT to describe the real, the factual, the true situation of a small child? Whenever I try to do this I am confronted with arguments that all serve the same purpose: that of not having to acknowledge the situation, of rendering it invisible, or, at best, of describing it as purely "subjective." The victim is always subjective, I am told: He knows only the wrong done to him, not *why* it was done to him, especially when that victim is a child, for how much can a child really understand? How should he be able to assess the overall situation—for instance, understand the plight of his parents and realize how greatly he has provoked their violence? Again and again the child's share of the blame is looked for and found, with the result that only in extremely brutal cases is the term "child abuse" mentioned, and even then with reservations, while the broad spectrum of psychic mistreatment is disputed or even totally denied. In this way the victims' voices are silenced almost before they are raised, and the truth, the whole *objective* truth, of the facts remains in obscurity.

The absurd consequences to which this silencing can lead could be observed in connection with an issue of the German magazine *Stern* published in 1987. When the son of the infamous mass murderer Hans Frank, the Nazi governor-general in Poland from 1939 to 1945, condemned his father's crimes outright, without embellishing, forgiving, or qualifying them and without acknowledging any blame for his report, he unleashed a wave of anger and indignation. Readers wrote, among other things: "No matter what Hans Frank may have done, his foulest deed was undoubtedly the procreation of this perverse monster of a son." "Anyone else is free to, should, in fact, write this article, but not the son. In doing so he acts just as inhumanly as his father once did." So we are told that it is inhuman and utterly loathsome if a child of a mass murderer is not prepared to idealize his father, to withhold the truth, and to betray himself.

The public forum is not, of course, the most helpful place to conduct a profitable confrontation with one's parents. If we are to allow the feelings of childhood to be revived, we need an enlightened witness and not the pent-up, undigested hatred of formerly abused children who, as adults, totally identify with the perpetrators. To expose oneself defenselessly to public view while harbor-

97

ing such feelings from childhood can amount to a kind of self-inflicted punishment, something one seeks when, in spite of everything, one still feels guilty at having expressed the criticism and is prepared to accept hate reactions as a well-deserved punishment. Many sons and daughters come to grief over their attempts at confrontation, either by exposing themselves to the cruelty of the public, just as they were once at the mercy of ignorant, unempathic parents, or, to court public favor, by assuring readers that they forgive their abusive parents everything.

However, according to Niklas Frank's statements, in publishing this report he was intent not on a personal accounting or private catharsis but on political action. He wished to show what his father had done, and what other fathers had done at the same time, and to show that their actions had been without a twinge of conscience but accompanied by a plethora of empty words. The son's statements might help some people to recognize the lies —unperceived because they are so familiar—that surround us. But although he may have succeeded in a few cases, many people still tried to suppress the truth by every possible means, even by publicly siding with the mass murderer against his child.

The tragedy is that this suppression is not at all necessary, for the power of the adult over the child—a power in existence for thousands of years—is so great that it functions perfectly without any additional sanction. In my generation the child learned to identify completely with the parents' perspective and never to question it. In the works of all the authors I know, I have observed that, despite occasional rebellion, they end up defending their parents against their own accusations. Accusations against parents are often associated with mortal fears, not only because of real threats but because a small child feels he is in deadly danger if he loses the love of the person closest to him. Thus the old repressed fear is preserved in the adult, and the danger signals stored so long ago can remain effective for a lifetime.

From a twelve-year-old boy I learned how completely a child of that age can feel total solidarity with an adult, although, unlike an adult, he is still capable of observing incriminating facts. The incident took place in a restaurant. The boy was listening as I discussed with a teacher the new corporal punishment law in the canton of Zurich. We were both indignant that corporal punishment of children, which had been abolished, was reintroduced in 1985 with the proviso "When the teacher is provoked by the pupil." We both felt that this proviso opened the door to legal abuse since a teacher could always claim that a pupil provoked him and since such a claim need be examined only by the school authorities, not by the court. That a school usually defends and protects the individual teacher is well known.

Our discussion of this law interested the boy, whom we did not know but who happened to be sitting at our table, and he suddenly exclaimed: "But there are cases where a pupil really does provoke the teacher, and then he must be punished!" We asked him whether he could remember such a case, and he replied that, yes, something like that had recently happened in his class. One of the boys had disrupted the lesson and had to be sent out of the room. I asked him what had led up to the pupil's behavior. The boy remembered exactly: The teacher had accused the pupil of something that had been done not by that boy but by someone else. The accused pupil didn't want to betray his classmate but kept protesting his own innocence. The teacher didn't believe him. That had incensed the pupil. I suggested that this was probably the cause of the subsequent provocation. To this the boy reacted with great indignation, saying that a teacher can be wrong and make a mistake: Allowances must be made for that, and no one should assume the right to disrupt the class.

This unqualified siding with the adult is probably no exception among good students, and no more so than their empathy with their parents. The following passage by the nineteenth-century German writer Wilhelm von Kügelgen is a particularly clear illustration of the degree to which denial and humiliation of the self can go hand in hand with this empathy:

In her personality my mother remained constant. It was not in her nature to show the tenderness she felt in her heart; she never dallied with me and never tolerated any naughtiness on my part, yet on the other hand she never alarmed me with moods or outbursts, and she made me feel that nobody in the world loved me more than she did. As the supreme reward for exceptional virtue I could expect a kiss on my brow from her, and this kiss was of such overpowering effect that it was always immediately apparent to my father when he entered the room.

My mother rarely punished, but she always attempted to make me fully appreciate my wrongdoing, and her homilies were so effective that I invariably felt ashamed and only too willing to offer an abject apology. To this day I am grateful to her for this method, inasmuch as it taught me to eradicate those remnants in my conscience that can be so detrimental to the frankness of one's character. On those occasions when it was necessary for me to do more serious penance for a transgression, I would be chained for an hour or so to the leg of a

100

table or chair, albeit merely by a thread, a thread which, however, I never dared break, so great was my respect for my
mother, nor did she undo these fetters even upon the arrival of
visitors. Or, depending on the degree of the transgression, she
would attach to my head a pair of long ass's ears made of stiff
music paper, and I was obliged to continue wearing these even
during dinner or supper.

As soon as my good Papa came into the dining room he was
able, of course, to recognize those Midas ears with even less
effort than that kiss on the brow, and he then had a way of
endowing his noble features with an expression of such distress that I always felt pierced to the heart. On one occasion
especially, when, due to a toothache, he appeared with a ban-
dage around his face, that expression moved me to tears. Poor
Papa! Not only was he in pain, but he had to endure such
disgrace on account of his son! I was unable to swallow a
mouthful, although we were having steamed noodles prepared
according to a genuine Bavarian recipe; but my mother made
me keep on the ears.

I owe this quotation to a reader who, in his accompanying letter, wrote that it was a horrifying example of the
correctness of my thesis. Presumably he meant the thesis
that the adult remembers the humiliations he suffered as
being a necessary measure for his own good and dog-
gedly clings to the notion of having been loved by the
parents who tormented him.

Even people who have enjoyed a worldwide reputation
for their intelligence succumbed to this error inasmuch
as they kept their true knowledge hidden as if under lock
and key. Thus, for instance, did Arthur Schopenhauer
write about his father:

My excellent father was . . . a strict and vehement man but
of perfect integrity, probity, and unswerving loyalty, at the

same time gifted with remarkable judgment in business matters. I can scarcely express in words how much I owe to him.
. . . Hence I shall always, as long as I live, retain in my heart
those inexpressible merits and acts of kindness of the best of
fathers and ever hold his memory sacred.

This "best of fathers" once wrote to his twelve-year-
old son Arthur:

It is my desire that you learn to make people look upon you
with favor. . . . And as for your walking erect and sitting up
straight: I advise you to ask any of your companions to administer you a slap should you let yourself be caught overlooking
this important matter. This is how the children of princes
acted, not shirking the short-lived pain, so as to avoid appear-
ing boorish for the rest of their lives. Nothing but this will
help.

A child who is not intimidated does not sit hunched
over at table. But a child who has had to accept the blows
and scolding of his "strict and vehement" father with
feelings of love will often be unable to get rid of his
spinal curvature for the rest of his life since that remains
the sole expression of his fear. Fresh blows cannot correct the bent posture, but they can transform it into an
upright, rigid armor that expresses not the truth of the
victim but rather the lie of the persecutor now newly
created.

Franz Kafka is among the few writers of his day who
were able to question their parents' behavior. In a letter
to his father of more than a hundred pages he tried to
submit his complaints, to articulate his anguish and make
it intelligible to his father. Although his father never read
that letter, Kafka did write it, and in it he made statements that in their discernment went far beyond that

which people in similar situations are allowed to express. I asked myself what made it possible for Franz Kafka— who, as his works and diaries show, was deprived at a very early age of human warmth, true affection, reassurance, and protection—to define his situation and be aware of his suffering. I asked myself this because I know that mistreated and severely neglected children who have known nothing but cruelty and violence simply do not doubt the appropriateness of such treatment. But Kafka was fortunate in his puberty to have a sister, Ottla, nine years his junior, who was the first to make him feel that he was worth loving. From that experience he realized that it was not his fault that he had been deprived of love, but it was simply and solely because his parents did not love him.

Ottla's sensitivity and understanding made it possible for Franz Kafka to be critical of their parents, but this criticism did not go beyond the intellectual level. He never reached the point of experiencing the feelings that would have pierced the armor of self-accusation and replaced depression and physical illness by a genuine rebellion. Although in his long letter to his father Kafka succeeded in describing how the father dealt with his child, he did not bring about his own liberation because ultimately he betrayed even the child that he was. By occupying the position of the adult and reproaching the child, once again depriving the child of speech, he failed the child. The father relativized what his son said and ridiculed him. The son was ready, in the end, to agree with his father: "Of course, in real life things cannot fit together as neatly as do the proofs in my letter."

In the conclusion to that letter I see Kafka's dependence on our value system, in which a consistent and

103

precise accusation directed at the parents, one that does not skirt realities, is considered one of the greatest sins. Franz Kafka remained loyal to this value system, although in many places he was close, at least intellectually, to seeing through its unethical, child-inimical character. Yet he never risked an emotional confrontation with his parents. A victim of his guilt feelings, he contracted tuberculosis and died of it at the age of forty-one.*

Countless examples in literature can demonstrate how difficult it is to see and define the obvious guilt of one's own parents. I would like to single out Eugene O'Neill's play *Long Day's Journey into Night* and quote at length from it to give the reader some insight into the situation of the adult son within the family. Presumably on the basis of pure intuition, the author uncovers relationships that explain why, in one family, the oldest son becomes an alcoholic, the second dies in childhood (before the play opens), and the youngest will die of tuberculosis. Whether O'Neill himself could clearly see the causes he points out is hard to say. I am more inclined to assume that, like the twelve-year-old boy I previously quoted, he was able to point out the causes but would have denied his knowledge had he been directly challenged. My as-

---

* With these references I do not want to encourage anyone to display his childhood feelings in public and expect to derive a therapeutic effect as a result, for that will certainly not materialize. Nor does great literary success provide any solution to anguish rooted in childhood, since the exposure of this anguish to the public, even an applauding one, does not promote the working through and the dissolving of childhood feelings. On the contrary, it blocks such a process and can finally render it impossible. However, I believe that the *results* of our own discoveries, the data that we have derived from our childhood feelings, should definitely be communicated so that the public may awake from its sleep. See also Miller, *Thou Shalt Not Be Aware*, pp. 242ff.

sumption is based on the fact that the author has por-
trayed the sons' fate with intellectual insight but without
the sympathy and pity that are palpable in his portrayal
of the parents. This solidarity with the *parents as victims* is
shared with the author by the characters in the play.
Although the sons are critical and capable of articulating
their reproaches, they never relinquish the perspective
of their parents. At heart they see their fate as their own
failure, about which they feel guilty. They understand,
and *want* to understand, why their father has become so
miserly. They love him and are prepared to make allowances for everything he does. It is only they themselves
whom they can forgive nothing. They are not allowed to
understand why they have become what they are. Yet
because everything the parents do seems so understandable to them, the sons can find no cause, no reason, for
their anger. Their warranted anger is repressed, and in
this repressed form it festers to the point of total self-
destruction in disease and addiction.

I quote here the long conversation between the father,
Tyrone, and the youngest son, Edmund, in the fourth
act. It reveals Edmund's desperate, lonely struggle for
the truth, against the lie, against conventional empty
phrases, against threadbare façades, and against denial
of realities. And at the same time it reveals why this
struggle is doomed to failure: Edmund is always alone.
Whatever he tries to express, he is never listened to. All
that is left to him is his own sympathy for this aging,
ignorant child who calls himself his father.

TYRONE
(*Goaded into vindictiveness.*)
Or for that matter, if you insist on judging things by what

she [Mary, Edmund's mother] says when she's not in her right mind, if you hadn't been born she'd never—

(He stops ashamed.)

EDMUND

(Suddenly spent and miserable.)

Sure, I know that's what she feels, Papa.

TYRONE

(Protests penitently.)

She doesn't! She loves you as dearly as ever mother loved a son! I only said that because you put me in such a God-damned rage, raking up the past, and saying you hate me—

. . .

You mustn't let yourself be too downhearted, lad, by the bad news you had today. Both the doctors promised me, if you obey orders at this place you're going, you'll be cured in six months, or a year at most.

EDMUND

(His face hard again.)

Don't kid me. You don't believe that.

TYRONE

(Too vehemently.)

Of course I believe it! Why shouldn't I believe it when both Hardy and the specialist—?

EDMUND

You think I'm going to die.

TYRONE

That's a lie! You're crazy!

EDMUND

(More bitterly.)

So why waste money? That's why you're sending me to a state institution—

TYRONE

(*In guilty confusion.*)

What state institution? It's the Hilltown Sanatorium, that's all I know, and both doctors said it was the best place for you.

EDMUND

(*Scathingly.*)

For the money! That is, for nothing, or practically nothing. Don't lie, Papa! You know damned well Hilltown Sanatorium is a state institution!

. . .

You can't deny it's the truth about the state institution, can you?

TYRONE

It's not true the way you look at it! What if it is run by the state? That's nothing against it. The state has the money to make a better place than any private sanatorium. And why shouldn't I take advantage of it? It's my right—and yours. We're residents. I'm a property owner. I help to support it. I'm taxed to death—

EDMUND

(*With bitter irony.*)

Yes, on property valued at a quarter of a million.

. . .

Don't lie about it!

(*With gathering intensity.*)

God, Papa, ever since I went to sea and was on my own, and found out what hard work for little pay was, and what it felt like to be broke, and starve, and camp on park benches because I had no place to sleep, I've tried to be fair to you because I knew what you'd been up against as a kid. I've tried to make allowances. Christ, you have to make allowances in this damned family or go nuts! I have

107

tried to make allowances for myself when I remember all the rotten stuff I've pulled! I've tried to feel like Mama that you can't help being what you are where money is concerned. But God Almighty, this last stunt of yours is too much! It makes me want to puke! Not because of the rotten way you're treating me. To hell with that! I've treated you rottenly, in my way, more than once. But to think when it's a question of your son having consumption, you can show yourself up before the whole town as such a stinking old tightwad! Don't you know Hardy will talk and the whole damned town will know! Jesus, Papa, haven't you any pride or shame?

(Bursting with rage.)

And don't think I'll let you get away with it! I won't go to any damned state farm just to save you a few lousy dollars to buy more bum property with! You stinking old miser—!

(He chokes huskily, his voice trembling with rage, and then is shaken by a fit of coughing.)

TYRONE

(Has shrunk back in his chair under this attack, his guilty contrition greater than his anger. He stammers.)

Be quiet! Don't say that to me! You're drunk! I won't mind you. Stop coughing, lad. You've got yourself worked up over nothing. Who said you had to go to this Hilltown place? You can go anywhere you like. I don't give a damn what it costs. All I care about is to have you get well. Don't call me a stinking miser, just because I don't want doctors to think I'm a millionaire they can swindle.

*(*EDMUND *has stopped coughing. He looks sick and weak. His father stares at him frightenedly.)*

You look weak, lad. You'd better take a bracer.

108

And now, since the father cannot exert power, since he has no argument left to support the lie, since the son is not so easily diverted from the truth, the last weapon is brought into play: The father appeals to his son's pity and understanding; he forgets his son's disease and submerges himself entirely in his own childhood. It may be assumed that this weapon has never missed its mark in the case of one's own child. The child immediately forgets his own anguish and inevitably becomes the support of the parents who are totally immersed in their own suffering.

EDMUND
(Grabs the bottle and pours his glass brimfull—weakly.)
Thanks.
(He gulps down the whiskey.)
TYRONE
(Pours himself a big drink, which empties the bottle, and drinks it. His head bows and he stares dully at the cards on the table— vaguely.)
Whose play is it?
(He goes on dully, without resentment.)
A stinking old miser. Well, maybe you're right. Maybe I can't help being. . . . It was at home I first learned the value of a dollar and the fear of the poorhouse. I've never been able to believe in my luck since. I've always feared it would change and everything I had would be taken away. But still, the more property you own, the safer you think you are. That may not be logical, but it's the way I have to feel. Banks fail, and your money's gone, but you think you can keep land beneath your feet.
(Abruptly his tone becomes scornfully superior.)

You said you realized what I'd been up against as a boy.
The hell you do! How could you? You've had everything
—nurses, schools, college, though you didn't stay there.
You've had food, clothing. Oh, I know you had a fling of
hard work with your back and hands, a bit of being home-
less and penniless in a foreign land, and I respect you for
it. But it was a game of romance and adventure to you. It
was play.

EDMUND

(Dully sarcastic.)

Yes, particularly the time I tried to commit suicide at
Jimmie the Priest's, and almost did.

TYRONE

You weren't in your right mind. No son of mine would
ever— You were drunk.

EDMUND

I was stone cold sober. That was the trouble. I'd stopped
to think too long.

TYRONE

(With drunken peevishness.)

Don't start your damned atheist morbidness again! I
don't care to listen. I was trying to make plain to you—
(Scornfully.)

What do you know of the value of a dollar? When I was
ten my father deserted my mother and went back to
Ireland to die. Which he did soon enough, and deserved
to, and I hope he's roasting in hell. He mistook rat poison for flour, or sugar, or something. There was gossip it
wasn't by mistake but that's a lie. No one in my family
ever—

EDMUND

My bet is, it wasn't by mistake.

TYRONE

More morbidness! Your brother put that in your head.

110

The worst he can suspect is the only truth for him. But never mind. My mother was left, a stranger in a strange land, with four small children, me and a sister a little older and two younger than me. My two older brothers had moved to other parts. They couldn't help. They were hard put to it to keep themselves alive. There was no damned romance in our poverty. Twice we were evicted from the miserable hovel we called home, with my mother's few sticks of furniture thrown out in the street, and my mother and sisters crying. I cried, too, though I tried hard not to, because I was the man of the family. At ten years old! There was no more school for me. I worked twelve hours a day in a machine shop, learning to make files. A dirty barn of a place where rain dripped through the roof, where you roasted in summer, and there was no stove in winter, and your hands got numb with cold, where the only light came through two small filthy windows, so on grey days I'd have to sit bent over with my eyes almost touching the files in order to see! You talk of work! And what do you think I got for it? Fifty cents a week! It's the truth! Fifty cents a week! And my poor mother washed and scrubbed for the Yanks by the day, and my older sister sewed, and my two younger stayed at home to keep the house. We never had clothes enough to wear, nor enough food to eat. Well I remember one Thanksgiving, or maybe it was Christmas, when some Yank in whose house mother had been scrubbing gave her a dollar extra for a present, and on the way home she spent it all on food. I can remember her hugging and kissing us and saying with tears of joy running down her tired face: "Glory be to God, for once in our lives we'll have enough for each of us!"

(He wipes tears from his eyes.)

111

A fine, brave, sweet woman. There never was a braver or finer.

EDMUND

(*Moved.*)

Yes, she must have been.

TYRONE

Her one fear was she'd get old and sick and have to die in the poorhouse.

(*He pauses—then adds with grim humor.*)

It was in those days I learned to be a miser. A dollar was worth so much then.

. . .

(*Vehemently.*)

You can choose any place you like! Never mind what it costs! Any place I can afford. Any place you like—within reason.

(*At this qualification, a grin twitches* EDMUND's *lips. His resentment has gone. His father goes on with an elaborately offhand, casual air.*)

There was another sanatorium the specialist recommended. He said it had a record as good as any place in the country. It's endowed by a group of millionaire factory owners, for the benefit of their workers principally, but you're eligible to go there because you're a resident. There's such a pile of money behind it, they don't have to charge much. It's only seven dollars a week but you get ten times that value.

(*Hastily.*)

I don't want to persuade you to anything, understand. I'm simply repeating what I was told.

EDMUND

(*Concealing his smile—casually.*)

Oh, I know that. It sounds like a good bargain to me. I'd like to go there. So that settles that.

(Abruptly he is miserably desperate again—dully.)

It doesn't matter a damn now, anyway. Let's forget it!

(Changing the subject.)

How about our game? Whose play is it?

TYRONE

(Mechanically.)

I don't know. Mine, I guess. No, it's yours.

(EDMUND *plays a card. His father takes it. Then about to play from his hand, he again forgets the game.)* Yes, maybe life overdid the lesson for me, and made a dollar worth too much, and the time came when that mistake ruined my career as a fine actor.

(Sadly.)

I've never admitted this to anyone before, lad, but to-night I'm so heartsick I feel at the end of everything, and what's the use of fake pride and pretense.

. . .

EDMUND

(Moved, stares at his father with understanding—slowly.)

I'm glad you've told me this, Papa. I know you a lot better now.

TYRONE

(With a loose, twisted smile.)

Maybe I shouldn't have told you. Maybe you'll only feel more contempt for me. And it's a poor way to convince you of the value of a dollar.

(Then as if this phrase automatically aroused an habitual association in his mind, he glances up at the chandelier disapprovingly.)

The glare from those extra lights hurts my eyes. You don't mind if I turn them out, do you? We don't need

them, and there's no use making the Electric Company
rich.

EDMUND

(*Controlling a wild impulse to laugh—agreeably.*)

No, sure not. Turn them out.

TYRONE

(*Gets heavily and a bit waveringly to his feet and gropes uncer-
tainly for the lights—his mind going back to its line of thought.*)

No, I don't know what the hell it was I wanted to buy.
(*He clicks out one bulb.*)

On my solemn oath, Edmund, I'd gladly face not having
an acre of land to call my own, nor a penny in the bank—
(*He clicks out another bulb.*)

I'd be willing to have no home but the poorhouse in my
old age if I could look back now on having been the fine
artist I might have been.

(*He turns out the third bulb, so only the reading lamp is on, and
sits down again heavily.* EDMUND *suddenly cannot hold back a
burst of strained, ironical laughter.* TYRONE *is hurt.*)

What the devil are you laughing at?

EDMUND

Not at you, Papa. At life. It's so damned crazy.

TYRONE

(*Growls.*)

More of your morbidness! There's nothing wrong with
life. It's we who—
(*He quotes.*)

"The fault, dear Brutus is not in our stars, but in ourselves that we are underlings."

. . .

EDMUND

You've just told me some high spots in your memories.
Want to hear mine? They're all connected with the sea.

Here's one. When I was on the Squarehead square rig-
ger, bound for Buenos Aires. Full moon in the Trades.
The old hooker driving fourteen knots. I lay on the bow-
sprit, facing astern, with the water foaming into spume
under me, the masts with every sail white in the moonlight, towering high above me. I became drunk with the
beauty and singing rhythm of it, and for a moment I lost
myself—actually lost my life. I was set free! I dissolved in
the sea, became white sails and flying spray, became
beauty and rhythm, became moonlight and the ship and
the high dim-starred sky! I belonged, without past or
future, within peace and unity and a wild joy, within
something greater than my own life, or the life of Man, to
Life itself! . . . Then the moment of ecstatic freedom
came. The peace, the end of the quest, the last harbor,
the joy of belonging to a fulfillment beyond men's lousy,
pitiful, greedy fears and hopes and dreams! . . . For a
second there is meaning! Then the hand lets the veil fall
and you are alone, lost in the fog again, and you stumble
on toward nowhere, for no good reason!
(He grins wryly.)
It was a great mistake, my being born a man, I would
have been much more successful as a sea gull or a fish. As
it is, I will always be a stranger who never feels at home,
who does not really want and is not really wanted, who
can never belong, who must always be a little in love with
death!

TYRONE
(Stares at him—impressed.)
Yes, there's the makings of a poet in you all right.
(Then protesting uneasily.)
But that's morbid craziness about not being wanted and
loving death.

115

EDMUND

(Sardonically.)

The *makings* of a poet. No, I'm afraid I'm like the guy who is always panhandling for a smoke. He hasn't even got the makings. He's got only the habit. I couldn't touch what I tried to tell you just now. I just stammered. That's the best I'll ever do. I mean, if I live. Well, it will be faithful realism, at least. Stammering is the native eloquence of us fog people.

Edmund calls himself one of the fog people, a beggar who is always "panhandling for a smoke," and with that he means poetry. Stammering as the primeval language of fog people? Here every word yields a meaning, if we bear in mind that from the very beginning Edmund was forbidden to see the truth, to sense it clearly, and to express it. He suspected that he was an unwanted child, he knew he didn't feel at home anywhere, but neither of those things is he allowed to say. His father calls him "morbid and crazy" when the son tries to describe his anguish, although Tyrone has heard from Mary that she resented her son's birth. What is left for the son other than stammering, fog, poetry, and finally death? His knowledge is banished; his parents relentlessly talk him out of it. There is nobody with whom he can share it.

O'Neill knew that in this play he had described his own past, as is shown by his dedication:

For Carlotta, on our 12th Wedding Anniversary

Dearest: I give you the original script of this play of old sorrow, written in tears and blood. A sadly inappropriate gift, it would seem, for a day celebrating happiness. But you will understand. I mean it as a tribute to your love and tenderness which gave me the faith in love that enabled me to face my dead at last and write this play—write it with deep pity and understanding and forgiveness for *all* the four haunted Tyrones.

These twelve years, Beloved One, have been a Journey into Light—into love. You know my gratitude. And my love!

GENE

Tao House
July 22, 1941.

But pity, understanding, and forgiveness "for *all* the four haunted Tyrones" were not enough to enable the author to save the real child from emotional death, the child who could not yet understand and was a mute victim of his parents' homelessness and pretense. In O'Neill's unconscious, the small, emotionally destroyed child he had once been lived on. In the play, that child shows up in Mary's beloved son who died as a baby and to whom the author gave his own name, Eugene. Eugene is the dead child between two brothers, the alcoholic Jamie and the consumptive poet Edmund, and is at the same time a symbol of O'Neill's fate. The brothers act out the destiny of Mary's father, an alcoholic who died of consumption, which she denies; and little Eugene, who had to die as a baby, represents the emotional death of the child who knows the truth. Actually all three brothers represent different sides of the single child who was sacrificed to the mother's lie, the child whom Eugene O'Neill evidently carried within himself. O'Neill displayed to the audience both the parents' lies and the son's truth. The audience is allowed to see them; only the son is denied access to the truth.

The last word in the play is given to the mother, Mary, who describes her tragedy. Not the true tragedy, not the fate of a little girl whose father was consumptive and alcoholic. No, that prosaic story must not even be mentioned; no one in the family is allowed to speak of it. What Mary expresses at the end of the play, with tender emotion and obviously supported by the author's sympathy, is an exalted, superficial version of her life: She had wanted to enter a convent and serve the Blessed Virgin, but Mother Elizabeth told her she must put herself to a test. "That was in the winter of senior year. Then in the spring something happened to me. Yes, I remember. I fell in love with James Tyrone and was so happy for a time."

These words bring the play to an end with a sentimental reassurance for the audience, who for more than three hours have been presented with nothing but the truth. But this truth is not allowed to prevail. The ending clouds it, and what remains is fogged over: Life is hard but at the same time beautiful. I did not enter the convent, but I did find my husband, whom I loved. We had children. We can be thankful that we were, after all, granted so much.

Mary doesn't ask: Why did I want to enter the convent? Why did I become an addict and lose control? Why are my sons being destroyed? She is not allowed to ask these questions. She must remain mired in confusion, in fog, in the complete idealization of her father, to the point where she refuses to acknowledge her son's consumption, explaining away his cough as a summer cold and absolutely forbidding any mention of her father's disease and alcoholism. We learn about these things only from her husband in her absence: her father was a great, generous, noble man who, according to Mary, loved her above all else and always protected her. Can the beloved daughter of a generous, noble man become an addict who destroys, must destroy, the life of her family? Such a girl has never existed nor ever can exist. And Mary is not this girl. In reality she is one of those countless girls who, at all costs and at all times, proclaim as reality the fairy tale of their father's splendid character. She will continue all her life to maintain that black is white and white is black, oblivious to the fact that in doing so she is driving not only herself but also her sons into madness. For a child who is exposed day after day to such confusion cannot elude it. He needs his mother, he wants to, has to, believe her. So he must deny his own observations and seek help in alcohol or other addictions or illness if there is no one to help him see the truth and bear it.

The following scene shows how Mary evades reality and how she, the "loving" mother, refuses to feel for her son even in the face of death, simply because the truth might bring her too close to the repressed pain that she fears. "You really ought to show more consideration," she bids Edmund, exactly as she was once bidden. And the adult Edmund tries, although feebly, to rebel against such bidding, but no one helps him, no one confirms his observations, so his attempts are doomed to failure, as they were, to an even greater extent, in his childhood. In those days the child did *everything* to conform to his mother's wish; he even gave up his health in his hope to become, like little Eugene, the mourned, one and only loved dead child of his mother. I know of no passage that depicts an impotent mother's power and abuse of power with greater penetration than the following one.

EDMUND

. . .

Listen, Mama. I'm going to tell you whether you want to hear or not. I've got to go to a sanatorium.

119

MARY

(*Dazedly, as if this was something that had never occurred to her.*)
Go away?
(*Violently.*)
No! I won't have it! How dare Doctor Hardy advise such
a thing without consulting me! How dare your father
allow him! What right has he? You are my baby! Let him
attend to Jamie!
(*More and more excited and bitter.*)
I know why he wants you sent to a sanatorium. To take
you from me! He's always tried to do that. He's been
jealous of every one of my babies! He kept finding ways
to make me leave them. That's what caused Eugene's
death. He's been jealous of you most of all. He knew I
loved you most because—

EDMUND

(*Miserably.*)
Oh, stop talking crazy, can't you, Mama! Stop trying to
blame him. And why are you so against my going away
now? I've been away a lot, and I've never noticed it broke
your heart!

MARY

(*Bitterly.*)
I'm afraid you're not very sensitive, after all.
(*Sadly.*)
You might have guessed, dear, that after I knew you knew
—about me—I had to be glad whenever you were where
you couldn't see me.

EDMUND

(*Brokenly.*)
Mama! Don't!
(*He reaches out blindly and takes her hand—but he drops it
immediately, overcome by bitterness again.*)

120

All this talk about loving me—and you won't even listen when I try to tell you how sick—

MARY

(With an abrupt transformation into a detached bullying mother-liness.)

Now, now. That's enough! I don't care to hear because I know it's nothing but Hardy's ignorant lies.

(He shrinks back into himself. She keeps on in a forced, teasing tone but with an increasing undercurrent of resentment.)

You're so like your father, dear. You love to make a scene out of nothing so you can be dramatic and tragic.

(With a belittling laugh.)

If I gave you the slightest encouragement, you'd tell me next you were going to die—

EDMUND

People do die of it. Your own father—

MARY

(Sharply.)

Why do you mention him? There's no comparison at all with you. He had consumption.

(Angrily.)

I hate you when you become gloomy and morbid! I forbid you to remind me of my father's death, do you hear me?

EDMUND

(His face hard—grimly.)

Yes, I hear you, Mama. I wish to God I didn't!

(He gets up from his chair and stands staring condemningly at her —bitterly.)

It's pretty hard to take at times, having a dope fiend for a mother!

(She winces—all life seeming to drain from her face, leaving it

with the appearance of a plaster cast. Instantly EDMUND *wishes
he could take back what he has said. He stammers miserably.)*
Forgive me, Mama. I was angry. You hurt me.
*(There is a pause in which the foghorn and the ships' bells are
heard.)*

    MARY
*(Goes slowly to the windows at right like an automaton—looking
out, a blank, far-off quality in her voice.)*
Just listen to that awful foghorn. And the bells. Why is it
fog makes everything sound so sad and lost, I wonder?

    EDMUND
(Brokenly.)
I—I can't stay here. I don't want any dinner.
*(He hurries away through the front parlor. She keeps staring out
the window until she hears the front door close behind him. Then
she comes back and sits in her chair, the same blank look on her
face.)*

    MARY
(Vaguely.)
I must go upstairs. I haven't taken enough.
(She pauses—then longingly.)
I hope, sometimes, without meaning it, I will take an
overdose. I never could do it deliberately. The Blessed
Virgin would never forgive me, then.
(She hears TYRONE *returning.)* . . .

    TYRONE

. . .

Where's Edmund?

    MARY

. . .

He said he didn't want any dinner. He doesn't seem to
have any appetite these days.
(Then stubbornly.)

But it's just a summer cold.
(TYRONE *stares at her and shakes his head helplessly and pours himself a big drink and drinks it. Suddenly it is too much for her and she breaks out and sobs.*)
Oh, James, I'm so frightened!
(*She gets up and throws her arms around him and hides her face on his shoulder—sobbingly.*)
I know he's going to die!

TYRONE

Don't say that! It's not true! They promised me in six months he'd be cured.

MARY

You don't believe that! I can tell when you're acting! And it will be my fault. I should never have borne him. It would have been better for his sake. I could never hurt him then. He wouldn't have had to know his mother was a dope fiend—and hate her!

TYRONE

(*His voice quivering.*)
Hush, Mary, for the love of God! He loves you. He knows it was a curse put on you without your knowing or willing it. He's proud you're his mother!
(*Abruptly as he hears the pantry door opening.*)
Hush, now! Here comes Cathleen. You don't want her to see you crying.

In a fraction of a second Edmund is confronted with the hatred lurking behind his mother's "love" ("I forbid you to remind me of my father's death") and comes out with his knowledge, but the very next moment he takes back what he has said and apologizes to her although there is no reason why he should. The child's lack of rights usually doesn't strike us because we have grown up with it and regard it as proper. Only in literature can so much truth be shown, provided it is depicted as pure fantasy, as "smoke" or even as "morbid and crazy." Mary represents the poor confused woman, the naive girl, the victim of addiction, and arouses the audience's pity just because she is no longer a child but the mother. But she is a mother who cuts off her son from the chances of life: She disputes his accurate observations, confuses him, fakes love for him, and finally demands love and respect in return. A son can rarely survive this kind of "mother love" unscathed. Yet society is blind to just such injuries.

Solidarity with the parents' interests, as well as the betrayal of the child that is expressed in both Kafka's and O'Neill's work, although in very different ways, can be found in all the authors I know, even the notably "rebellious" ones. There are, of course, some writers, such as Beckett, Ionesco, and Genet, whose works lack this gesture of final reconciliation, but in those works it is not the parents, let alone the authors' own parents, who are being accused. It is society per se—parents in an abstract, more symbolic form. In all the works in which authors blame parents directly, however, the parents have the last word, and the child is silenced.

This turnabout can be very well observed in some of Ingmar Bergman's films. In *Fanny and Alexander* (1983) the child's repression centers on brutal child abuse. Perhaps a father's cruelty can be depicted so vividly in the film because he is the stepfather, while the benign, deceased father can be idealized in the background. Yet thanks to this dual role for the father characters Bergman succeeds in portraying the mendacious nature of child-rearing more faithfully than in any of his earlier films. Unfortunately Bergman takes this courageous step but follows it with the embellishing process to which the child is mercilessly delivered up because he cannot defend himself and would like to believe in the embellishment: The mother is kind, the family is kind, the irresponsible uncle loves life, and everything is rosy again. That the "loving" mother hands her children over to a criminal and forces them to respect and love him seems to have escaped Bergman's notice. So in the end the child remains alone, separated from his truth and, basically, abandoned by society as represented by the author and the audience.

Another example is offered by Arthur Miller's play *Death of a Salesman*. It is the story of a poor, not unlikable, simple man who was constantly suppressed by his parents and his able brother, with the result that as an adult he cannot get anywhere in his job. He spends all his life toiling away for his family, finally sacrificing his life so that the family can live off his insurance money: all in all, a quiet hero of our time. After the funeral, his widow and two sons take leave of him at his grave, with genuine grief, wistful memories, and deep gratitude. The unknown soldier, the unknown warrior of today's anonymous society. But what preceded this ending? It wasn't enough for the hopeless loser to have two sons who loved him; he needed brilliant sons of whom he could be proud so he could at last prove to his brother and his parents that he had amounted to something. The play shows that both sons are unable to develop the qualities they undeniably possess and are unable to live their lives because their one wish is to measure up to their father's expectations, and in this they never succeed. The play also shows that the sons can't possibly succeed, and why. Like O'Neill's play, it depicts the slow destruction of two young people, in this case more so by their father and their love for him. The sons completely idealize whatever the father has done, and the author himself succumbs to this idealization. He ends the play in such a way that the truth finally does become totally invisible. Did Arthur Miller show the whole truth? Yes. But was he in a position to *know* what he did? I must say that, having written such an ending, he almost certainly did not know what he had shown.

SEVEN

WITHOUT TRUTH THERE CAN BE NO HELP

A DANISH JOURNALIST sent me an article some years ago showing that in Denmark, too, children are still very often punished and beaten. In her accompanying letter she suggested that in the Afterword to *Thou Shalt Not Be Aware* I had probably overestimated the progress being made in Scandinavia, inasmuch as the evil was far from being eliminated there. She may be right—that it will be a very long time before there are no more battered children. But in my opinion a public outcry over it already amounts to progress, progress resulting in Scandinavia as well as in the United States from more humane legislation. The occasional articles on this subject in other countries are still a long way from constituting a public outcry.

In Switzerland, for example, attempts were made to enact legislation that would require doctors to report all cases of child abuse that came to their notice. Yet it was the pediatricians, child psychiatrists, family therapists, and experts in child abuse who were the very people to fight tooth and nail against such a law. They submitted a letter to the government of Switzerland setting out in detail, under the motto "Help rather than punish," the potential dangers of such a law.

This petition against a more humane law is a document of the first rank, which is why I am reproducing it here.

Dear Sir:

Through the press we have learned that the revised penal code will require that light bodily injuries as well as repeated assaults, particularly when perpetrated on children, be declared offenses requiring public prosecution.

Child abuse is a serious problem with which physicians have long had to deal. However, pediatricians were not represented on the study commission of experts and were granted no opportunity in the hearings to comment on the text of the new law.

On July 25, 1986, therefore, representatives (listed below) of university pediatric clinics and children's hospitals from all parts of Switzerland assembled for a conference. Based on their many years of experience and dealing with child abuse, they herewith take the liberty of declaring their stand with regard to this amendment to the penal code:

We appreciate your intention to offer children better protection with the new version of the aforementioned article of the penal code. Moreover, this corresponds to our aim to do everything possible to prevent assaults on children as well as

128

bodily harm, psychic injury, and neglect, or to avoid their repetition. However, we are unanimously and firmly convinced that it is scarcely possible to protect children from abuse by means of the penal code, and that consequently the planned amendment to the penal code will not bring about the desired improved protection. In our experience—which corresponds to worldwide experience—children are abused by parents who are in a state of affect and intense psychic tension, as well as under social pressure. In an extreme situation of this kind it is not to be expected that parents will allow themselves to be deterred from abusive action by provisions of the penal code.

In the last few years it has been recognized internationally that, in dealing with the specific problems of child abuse, measures taken on the principle of "Help rather than punish" have a much greater prospect of success, and that by this method the well-being of the abused child and his family can be better preserved. Following the example of other countries—notably Holland (Bureau of Medical Examiners), the Federal Republic of Germany (child protection agencies), and Scandinavia—children's hospitals and pediatricians in Switzerland have for the last ten to fifteen years also been working according to that principle. Thanks to this procedure, the number of reports, both voluntary and by outsiders, is steadily on the rise so that in many cases genuine family assistance can be offered in good time (if necessary in co-operation with civil law authorities).

The intended penal code reform would in our opinion have the following undesirable effects:

1. The number of voluntary reports (by parents, care persons, etc.) will decrease.

2. Mothers' counselors, kindergarten supervisors, and schoolteachers, as well as neighbors, will increasingly refrain from reporting their suspicions to specialized agencies. As a result, reports by outsiders will predictably also decline.

129

3. Pediatricians and other medical agencies will also be reluctant to express their suspicions of child abuse.

4. In some cases injured children will not be taken, or taken too late, to receive the necessary treatment.

5. The rehabilitation of the family may be hampered by criminal proceedings.

There is a great danger that, for fear of consequences to the family arising from criminal prosecution, all individuals and authorities will, when faced by cases of abuse, be increasingly hesitant and close their eyes to the suspected problem. This will mean less action on behalf of abused children, with less possibility of helping them. Yet, in spite of the new legislation, the number of abuses will not decrease.

For the above reasons we would urge you to reconsider the proposed amendment. We would greatly appreciate being granted an opportunity to submit our views in person.

Strangely enough, the experts wish to help the parents by sparing them the truth that they are inflicting lifelong damage on their children. They believe that in this way worse abuse can be prevented. But is there any validity whatever to this belief?

In the entire professional literature covering child abuse there is hardly any mention of the fact that parents beat their children to keep their own traumas repressed. Yet there is a steady stream of published works that call themselves scientific and are searching for the causes of child abuse. These studies give the impression of someone who puts on very dark sunglasses in bright sunshine and, flashlight in hand, goes looking for something that bystanders have no difficulty seeing. Similar sunglasses and blindfolds are used in the so-called therapy treatment of the parents: A great deal of understanding is shown for an unemployed father who beats his children.

There is no problem understanding an overburdened executive who does the same thing, especially when he is irritated by his wife. The wife also meets with understanding when she can't help beating her child after the milk boils over. This parental behavior is understood because the therapists have probably been victims of such situations countless times and are invariably ready to understand the parents rather than face the repressed truth about their own lives. They have been trained for this, and at the same time they have been taught that it is dangerous to become aware of the situation of the child.

In a circular letter issued by an association in Zurich called Parents in Distress, dated May 15, 1987, we read among other things:

An unsatisfactory partnership or disappointment over the parental role, as well as unacceptable and oppressive social situations caused by the behavior of the child, can exert unbearable psychic pressure on the parents.

With such bizarre notions do some social workers administer "therapy" to "poor" parents who have beaten their children half to death because they could no longer stand the children's behavior, of which they themselves were the cause.

Without correct information on the causes and consequences of child abuse, neither the parents nor the children can be helped. But this information will not be taken seriously until legislation ceases to evade the fact that child abuse is a serious crime, and until doctors are *compelled* to report such crimes. Legislation of this kind would entail changes that are long overdue. As I point out in the final pages of the Appendix, punishment need not mean imprisonment; what matters most is that par-

131

ents be helped *not* to ward off their own truth and thus be enabled to find their way out of the trap. The problem cannot be solved with high-sounding words about help. Some cases can be helped only if the guilty person is threatened with punishment, so that he may begin to have some inkling of what he has done and also of what was once done to him.

The only person who can be helped is one seeking help because he knows he is in trouble. But most parents who seriously abuse their children are barely conscious of the trouble they are in. Moreover, they have no guilt feelings because all they know from their childhood is similar treatment and because they have learned to regard such treatment as correct. They firmly believe that they beat their children and treat them cruelly so as to enable the children to develop noble characters, and they believe that they are providing their children with "sex initiation" when they use them to satisfy their own lust. Most incestuous fathers have difficulty grasping that their behavior is criminal. How can one "help" them without making them see this? And how can one make them see this as long as society is reluctant to describe crimes against children as offenses liable to public prosecution and to embody this in legislation? Parents who seek help in therapy or turn to parenting schools are already aware of the trouble they are in. But innumerable children are exposed to mortal danger with their parents because the parents are devoid of any guilty conscience. The only way to help these children is with new legislation that unequivocally classifies as criminal the parental behavior that has hitherto been regarded as completely normal.

Anyone who is not allowed to *condemn outright* what is

evil, perfidious, vile, perverse, and mendacious will always be lacking in orientation and compelled blindly to repeat his own experiences. Unfortunately this fact is not well known because it calls into question the traditional values of morality and religion. Almost all official agencies for the aid of abused children work on the confusing principle of "Help, not condemn," and constantly emphasize their nonjudgmental attitude. But this is the very attitude that makes it harder for the persons seeking help to liberate themselves from the compulsion to repeat their own history, a liberation that is possible only if the occurrence of abuse is deplored and the perpetrators condemned outright.

I know of a case of extreme perversion with sexual, sadistic, and religious elements that a father secretly inflicted on his daughter for years. When the affair came to light through the daughter's attempted suicide, the father completely denied his guilt. Prolonged therapy efforts did nothing to change his attitude; he insisted that he was innocent because after each sexual contact his daughter had forgiven him his "sin." Then an enlightened social worker succeeded in awakening in the father memories of his own childhood and the feelings connected with it. Bizarre sexual games with his mother began to surface, games with a compulsory ritual: The child had to act the part of the priest, forgiving his mother her sins and dispensing absolution. The man claimed that he had been "very happy" to do this because in those situations his mother had been quite humble and contrite and he had experienced this as a great relief from her otherwise very domineering nature. He was no longer aware that these scenes of absolution had been extremely frightening because they were so confusing and were merely the culmination of a series of abuses in which he had been physically and psychically raped and threatened to an almost intolerable degree. This part of his experiences remained repressed because the boy was at the mercy of his mother and because no witness stood up for him, with the result that any conscious, more comprehensive memory was denied him.

Yet years later the experiences stored up in his body induced the grown man to reenact the scenes of rape, threat, and forgiveness with his daughter. The absence of guilt feelings went hand in hand with the conviction that his mother, because she was a devout churchgoer, must also have been guiltless and actually had never done him any harm. It was only the discovery of his own traumas, the conscious experience of pain, anger, indignation, humiliation, and confusion, that enabled him to mourn what had happened. Only now was he able to mourn the fact that, with his repression, he had almost driven his daughter to her death, from which she escaped by a sheer miracle or coincidence. Only when he dared to recognize his mother's crimes against him was it no longer necessary for him to protect the mother by repeating those crimes against his daughter and pretending that his behavior was harmless.

Now that he knows the truth, this father will no longer be in danger of sexually abusing his child, whereas all practice at self-control had never succeeded in preventing him. Yet it is just such practices that are offered by parenting schools, accompanied by misleading assurances that the therapists "fully understand" such abuse and would never condemn it. I consider this attitude both wrong and confusing, supporting as it does the perpetrator's lack of insight. Every abuse of a child *must*

134

be condemned and is *not* "understandable." It can be explained only by the private perversion of the perpetrator's parents—not that this makes it in any way excusable. Only through the unequivocal condemnation of child abuse will society and the individual become aware of the true state of affairs and what it will lead to.

It must also be made clear that the problem does not merely affect a few aberrant families and individual perversions. Society must be shaken out of its sleep and be made to see that until now it has been sanctioning humanity's greatest crime. It is necessary to arouse the guilty conscience that can be completely absent even in cases of actual physical mutilation of small children. The common practice of circumcision shows how in many cultures the cruel mutilation of children's sexual organs is taken for granted. This practice is demanded by religious institutions and is not prevented by any legislation. Seventy-four million women are alive today whose clitoris was mutilated in childhood. The monstrous rationale for this was, among others, that the woman was not supposed to enjoy the sex act. With male circumcision the "reasons" vary from culture to culture, but common to all is the fictitious claim that circumcision is performed in the interests of the child. That this procedure constitutes a cruelty that will later encourage the adult to indulge in similar, also denied, cruelties and will invest his deeds with the legitimacy of a clear conscience is constantly overlooked and ignored, although some scientists have been able to refute all such "reasons" for circumcision. Desmond Morris, for example, writes:

For thousands of years, in many different cultures, the genitals have fallen victim to an amazing variety of mutilations and restrictions. For organs that are capable of giving us an immense amount of pleasure they have been given an inordinate amount of pain.

The commonest form of assault they have suffered is male and female circumcision. This strange mutilation is older than civilization and was probably already well established in the Stone Age. Although it is a piece of deliberate wounding of children by adults, it has always been done with the best of intentions. Over the millennia it has caused countless deaths from infection, but its advantages have always been said to outweigh the risks involved. These alleged advantages have varied from epoch to epoch and culture to culture, but recent re-examination of the evidence has shown that they are all imaginary.

It has been claimed that one of the oldest reasons for performing male circumcision—the removal of the foreskin—is that it provided immortality in the shape of life after death. This odd notion was based on the observation that when the snake sheds its skin it emerges with glistening new scales and is "reborn." If the snake can enjoy rebirth by the removal of skin, so too can the human being. For snake read penis; for snakeskin read foreskin.

Once male circumcision had become traditional it no longer mattered whether the old beliefs survived. Being circumcised was now a badge of belonging to a particular society. The ritual mutilation spread and spread. Ancient Egyptians were doing it as long ago as 4000 B.C. In the Old Testament, Abraham demanded it. Arabs circumcised as well as Jews. Mohammed was said to have been born without a foreskin (which he may well have been, as this condition is not unknown to medical science), a claim which automatically doomed the foreskins of his future male followers.

As the centuries passed, religious reasons gave way, for many, to quack medical arguments. The possession of a foreskin was said to cause "masturbatory insanity." Other medical

136

horrors resulting from its retention included hysteria, epilepsy, nocturnal incontinence, and nervousness. Such ideas survived into the early part of the present century and even led to the formation of an Orificial Surgery Society devoted exclusively to the "modification" of offending genitals as a means of preventing mental illness.

When at last this nonsense was on the decline a crisis arose. What new reason could be found for mutilating children's genitals? The solution had to be one that suited the rational climate of twentieth-century scientific enquiry. The answer appeared in that learned journal *The Lancet* in 1932: foreskins caused cancer! By the end of the 1930s 75 per cent of boys in the United States were being circumcised; by 1973 it was 84 per cent; by 1976 it was 87 per cent. Cancer had become the secular version of hellfire and brimstone, the perfect weapon for the anxiety-makers of a post-religious society.

To be more precise, the claim was that the "debris" called smegma which collects under retained foreskins could cause cancer of the penis and also cancer of the cervix of the wives of the uncircumcised. The paper which started this false rumour was founded on faulty statistics, but nobody minded because here was a plausible new reason for slicing away at the infantile penis. Subsequent experiments, however, revealed that there is nothing remotely carcinogenic about the smegma produced under the fold of the foreskin, but they were widely ignored. Other investigations showed that women whose uncircumcised husbands always wore condoms were no more or less likely to develop cervical cancer than those whose husbands never wore condoms. But, again, nobody wanted to know. In one project, a country where there was no circumcision at all was compared with one in which all males were circumcised. The results showed, to the relief of the foreskin snippers, that prostate cancer was higher in the uncircumcised country. Unfortunately this form of cancer is an ailment of elderly men, and when a correction for age distribution was made the figures showed that this disorder was actually more likely in the circumcised country.

Not only was the cancer scare completely without foundation, but the operation of foreskin removal continued to prove a distinct health hazard for small babies. There were many cases of haemorrhage, ulceration of the urethra, surgical trauma and local infection. In rare cases foreskin removal resulted in the death of the baby. There were also more subtle effects with possible long-term implications: following circumcision male babies showed an increase in the level of hormones related to stress; sleep patterns altered; there was more crying and more irritability.

Despite all this, "medical" circumcision continued (and still continues) at a merry pace in certain countries where private medicine is the rule. In Britain, significantly, there was a dramatic decline in the operation following the introduction of the National Health scheme and free treatment. It is impossible to refrain from asking why it should be that the operation sank to a level of less than one per cent (only 0.41 per cent of male babies in 1972) in a country where there was suddenly no financial gain to be made from it, while in the United States, for example, in the same year, over 80 per cent of male babies were circumcised, at an annual cost to health-insurance companies of more than $200 million. The new deities demanding foreskins appear to be more fiscal than sacred.

Young females have also been assaulted in a similar fashion. This has been rare in the West, although as recently as 1937 a Texas doctor was advocating the removal of the clitoris to *cure* frigidity. The harshest traditions of female circumcision are found in Africa, parts of the Middle East, Indonesia and Malaysia. It is a staggering fact that, far from being an ancient memory, the practice of cutting away all or part of the external genitals of young females is still going on in more than 20 countries.

No fewer than 74 million women alive today have been

subjected to this mutilation. In the worst cases they have had their labia and clitoris scraped or cut away and their vaginal opening stitched up with silk, catgut or thorns, leaving only a tiny opening for urine and menstrual blood. After the operation the girl's legs are bound together to ensure that scar-tissue forms and the condition becomes permanent. Later, when they marry, these females suffer the pain of having their artificially reduced orifices broken open by their husbands.

The effect of this practice is to dramatically reduce sexual pleasure for wives in the countries concerned, which may be its hidden significance. A side-effect is a high number of deaths and serious illnesses caused by the unhygienic conditions under which the operations are performed, especially in such countries as Oman, South Yemen, Somalia, Djibouti, Sudan, southern Egypt, Ethiopia, northern Kenya and Mali. The continuance of such practices in the twentieth century against a background of modern enlightenment is clearly going to puzzle historians of the distant future.

Historians and psychologists will long continue to ponder the reasons for this outlandish behavior because in their deliberations they overlook the only correct explanation. But in the long run this explanation cannot be avoided, and it becomes obvious the moment the question is asked: What eventually happens to the person who was mutilated as a child? When a small child is tortured by ignorant adults, won't he have to take his revenge later in life? He is bound to avenge himself unless his subsequent life allows the old wounds to heal in love, which is seldom the case. As a rule, children who were once injured will later injure their own children, maintaining that their behavior does no harm because their own loving parents did the same. Besides, in the case of circumcision it is a religious demand, and to many people it is still unthinkable that religion could demand cruelty.

But what if the unthinkable is true? Are the children and children's children to be sacrificed because of the ignorance of the priests? It took three hundred years for the church to accept Galileo's proofs and admit its error. Today it is not a matter of theoretical astronomical proofs but of the practical consequences deriving from an insight that could save humanity from self-destruction, *because it has already been proven that all destructive behavior has its roots in the repressed traumas of childhood.* As soon as legislators become serious about the rights of the child to protection and respect as proclaimed by UNESCO, the fact will have to be acknowledged that ritual circumcisions

1. offer no advantage and are a mutilation;
2. prevent the relaxation experience and lead to over-stimulation with potentially destructive and self-destructive effects;
3. inflict a trauma on the child leading to an injury of his whole being, with the consequences of these injuries affecting not only the individual and his descendants but other human beings as well.

Every criminal was once a victim, but not every victim necessarily becomes a criminal. It depends on whether an informed witness can help the victim to become aware of the cruelty experienced, that is, to feel and see the cruelty inflicted on him. Every adult criminal lacked this witness in his childhood; otherwise he would not have become a criminal (see the previous discussion in Chapter 2). But it is never too late for this witness to appear. Every crime is also a cry for help. Enlightened therapists, doctors, nurses, jurists, and teachers can become such rescuing witnesses as soon as they cease to evade the truth and in this manner help the criminal by helping the child in him. More humane legislation that no longer casts a veil over crimes is an essential requirement for this.

In pointing to the childhood of a criminal or mass murderer, I never do so to arouse pity for a monster but solely to describe the genesis of monsters and to show how an innocent child can be turned into an outright wicked person. Fortunately most people do not fall into this extreme category because they were privileged to salvage and develop some part of their good, humanitarian nature and to identify themselves—not completely but only partially and to varying degrees—with their attacker. As long as this part, the capacity for feeling and empathy, is not entirely destroyed, such people have more than one chance to give up denying their sufferings, to feel those sufferings, to recognize their true causes, and in this way liberate themselves from evil, from the compulsion to commit evil deeds.

Once able to feel their own misery they will also feel pity for the plight of others. They can be accompanied along this path by other people who, as enlightened witnesses, can confirm their observations and feelings, protect them from self-destruction, and give them a sense of their own empathy, but no more than that. The confrontation with his own past can be accomplished only by that person himself; no one can travel this path for him.

If someone had come to me and related the history of my childhood, in all the details I have since discovered, it would have had no effect whatever on me. I would have

141

believed it or not, but even if I had believed it, it would have meant no more to me than the story of a stranger, because it would not have been experienced. The only access that could truly help me to abandon my intellectual resistance opened up through the feelings of the very small child in me who was the sole witness to her mother's abuse. Why, then, was I able to give up the repression? Because I wanted at all costs to know the truth and finally did find a witness who helped me to search for that truth (I discuss this in detail in Chapter 1 of Part II).

Thanks to the encounter with my childhood, I know that neither education nor traditional therapy can genuinely eliminate destructive and self-destructive tendencies. For a while it might look as if they would, especially when the victims of the person in therapy remain silent. If that person himself is the victim he will be prevented by the medical establishment, often aided by unnecessary operations, from noticing what he is doing to himself. But sooner or later it becomes apparent that destruction of life gives rise only to new destruction as long as it has not been fully recognized. The once merciless behavior of parents bears fruit in their children, whom it in turn forces to deal with themselves and others just as mercilessly for as long as they evade the truth.

The Jungian doctrine of the shadow and the notion that evil is the reverse of good are aimed at denying the reality of evil. But evil is real. It is not innate but acquired, and it is never the reverse of good but rather its destroyer. Shakespeare was aware of this. He saw and showed the origins of evil but never tried to relativize evil by using psychological explanations, as is done in

142

psychoanalysis, for instance. Richard III, Macbeth, and some of his other characters are evil because they are destructive, even when we know why they have become so. Our knowledge cannot alter them. They can change only if they sense, not merely intellectually but with their feelings, how they have been turned into evil people. Only then will they be able to remove the blockages and, by experiencing the blocked pain, liberate the abused child who had no wish to harm anyone on coming into the world, the child who wanted to love but found no one to make that possible for him. All he found was barbed wire and walls on all sides, and he believed this to be the world. When he grew up he built gigantic worlds full of walls and barbed wire, or complicated philosophical and psychological systems, in the hope and expectation of receiving love in return, the love he never received from his parents when he was an "unworthy life." The so-called bad child becomes a bad adult and eventually creates a bad world. The loved child will create a different world, for it is our biological mandate to protect human life, not destroy it.

It is not true that evil, destructiveness, and perversion inevitably form part of human existence, no matter how often this is maintained. But it is true that we are daily producing more evil and, with it, an ocean of suffering for millions that is absolutely avoidable. When one day the ignorance arising from childhood repression is eliminated and humanity has awakened, an end can be put to this production of evil.

II

THE AWAKENING

ONE

MY PATH TO MYSELF

HOW DOES ONE arrive somewhere when, without knowing it, one has always been there? How does it happen that confusion turns into clarity, fear of pain into freedom to experience feelings; that volumes of empty words turn into simple facts, the constant flight-from-self into being-with-oneself; that blindness turns into vision, deafness into hearing, indifference into empathy, ignorant crime into informed responsibility, murderous lusts into calm, clenched despair into relaxation, self-destruction into self-protection, self-alienation into self-harmony? None of this happens by an effort of will, by sermons, with the aid of theories, and least of all with the

147

aid of medication. The effort of will can lead to even more clenched despair, moralizing to more effective denial, while medication and drugs can often lead to the causes of suffering remaining forever unknowable, the keys to the truth forever undiscoverable.

Some fifteen years ago, Arthur Janov gave an answer to all these questions by saying that it was enough to feel the primal pain and to discover the primal needs. This answer is not wrong, but it is not complete or precise enough, nor does it tell us how we are to go about feeling the primal pain. But it was not for this reason that it was smiled at by most "experts" and not taken seriously. The real reason was the uncomfortable nature of this reply. To many people it seems easier to take medication, to smoke, drink alcohol, preach, educate or treat others, and prepare wars than to expose themselves to their own painful truth.

For me it was not easier. Thanks to my painting I found myself on the path to my history, and nothing would induce me to turn back. That much was clear to me. Nevertheless, I came up against a barrier. I wanted to know what had happened in my early childhood, but I lacked the necessary tools. My training as a psychoanalyst was of no help to me. Free association kept me within the circle of intellectual resistance, the circle of my thoughts, assumptions, and hypotheses, the testing of which was denied me because my blocked feelings prevented any access to reality. I read books by Arthur Janov, and something told me that this man had found a crucial path, but it seemed to lack something that at the time I couldn't define.

In *The Primal Scream,* Janov describes how one of his patients suddenly became contorted with pain at the suggestion that he visualize his father and speak to him directly. Although after reading about Gestalt, encounter, Reich therapy, and bioenergetics, I was not exactly surprised by this discovery, the connection between that patient's childhood pain and his life history seemed to me to emerge much more clearly in his therapy with Janov than it would with all those other forms of therapy. This fascinated me, and it seemed reasonable enough to suppose that the experiencing of repressed events can lead to the abandoning of symptoms. But how to arrive at such experiencing, I wondered. Must one go to Los Angeles? If Janov really had discovered a universal truth, I thought, then the same logical sequence that was revealed in the accounts of his patients must be present in me too, and I should be able to discover it in myself. But how do I find someone to help me do this without irritating me with pedagogic opinions that he himself cannot see through?

I set out to look for this person and talked to a great many primal therapists in various countries. I established that there were many who can very quickly cast other people into the deepest despair, helplessness, and early-childhood fear. This part of the Janov technique spread like wildfire. But since this is not enough, since this is not full but only partial therapy, the dangers lurking in these turbulently released forces soon became evident. Although the experiencing of old pain provides relief on a physical level, the primal pain cannot be dissolved unless the individual steps on the other levels are taken. Many patients, therefore, remained in a perpetual state of unresolved feelings. Moreover, when the therapists found the emerging realities too much to bear, they resorted to the entire gamut of their education so as to preserve

149

their patients from the looming dangers of suicide or psychosis. Being at a loss, they began to combine their primal therapy with transactional analysis, or even with psychoanalytic concepts or religious content, a procedure that enabled them to restore their hastily destroyed defense at the expense of truth, but this time for good. Naturally, patients so treated were in a hurry to manage the feelings of others as quickly as possible and thus ward off their own helplessness and the *unresolved* emotional chaos in themselves. The procedure of rapidly putting people into a state of pain and describing this as therapy can also be a legal vent for suppressed sadistic impulses.

Then there were those who did not pretend to be therapists but quite frankly posed as gurus, abusing Janov's discovery to manipulate others in order to acquire love and large sums of money. Once confronted with feelings, their followers became addicted and remained dependent on the only guru who could satisfy this addiction. It was in his interest not to terminate this dependence so as not to forfeit the source of his power.

All these observations made me suspicious of primal therapy. Not that I was any longer in danger of being impressed by pedagogic tricks, let alone of joining a sect; but until I found a primal therapist with a clear, convincing therapy concept that coincided with my own insights, I seemed destined to remain stuck in a dead end, unless I were able to find the way out of this emotional confusion on my own. For me, a true therapy means a growing independence, and because I saw this possibility in the accounts of Janov's patients I was at first mystified as to why many of them joined sects. I couldn't understand how a person who has learned to be in touch with himself and to understand his own history could become a tool of alien interests. Yet the facts were undeniable. Did they, then, speak against this therapy? Or was Janov's therapy incomplete? If so, what was the missing piece? Could it be that the technique of releasing feelings, although it can be learned and passed on, is far from sufficient? Could it be that the success of therapy still depends on whether a patient can or cannot bear the truth about earlier abuses as it surfaces in his feelings? For to feel something momentarily, to sense something for a short time or even to know it intellectually, is a long way from enduring the truth permanently and integrating it.

When I see how many therapists still deny the truth about child abuse, I can imagine that an important part of the answer to my question is to be sought in that denial. Perhaps the child in the adult who has been encouraged to feel must escape into a sect once he discovers his past terrorization and cannot bear this truth on his own. For the patient to stop avoiding the reality that emerges in his pain, for him to dissolve the obstructive guilt feelings, he needs an environment that is unreservedly on the side of the child. Nowhere did I find this environment, not even among the primal therapists whom I met at that time. I found various people with varying backgrounds who, whenever I mentioned the innocence of the child and the guilt of the parents, at some point defended the parents.

At first I could hardly grasp that I should be completely alone with my insights but that nevertheless they could be true. I thought: If they all agree that a person can rid himself of symptoms only when he has forgiven his parents, how can I be sure that I am not mistaken?

151

The sum total of the experience of all the others must surely be far greater than mine. It was the reawakened memories of my mother's pedagogic terrorizing that finally gave me the key. It became clear to me that the consensus among the therapists arose not from their experience but from their education and that the forgiveness they take so much for granted and demand so unanimously must be unconditionally rejected because it is bound to prevent the success of any therapy.

In the many group discussions I conducted on this subject, almost all the therapists clung to the idea that one must forgive one's parents to get rid of one's symptoms. When my counterarguments seemed convincing, the most they would say was that, while they would not directly demand forgiveness, they would put it to the patient that he "would feel better" if he could forgive. They failed to notice that they were thus carrying on a pedagogic manipulation—one, moreover, whose purpose was to serve only traditional morality but not the interest of the patient, who was once an injured child and must confront the origin of those injuries. He will not achieve consciousness of past events until he recognizes that the morality exerted by his parents was life-negating and life-destroying. In aligning themselves with this morality, the therapists enter into the heritage of the pedagogues, who always take the side of the adults against the child. Not only do they reinforce the pernicious effect of pedagogy, but they obscure the process by calling what they do "therapy."

Needless to say, all parents of today's patients want to be forgiven every cruelty. The child was well aware of this, and his main concern was to fulfill this desire to satisfy his parents. Repressing his feelings made reconciliation possible. The cost was never known because the connection between repression and symptoms remained so long undiscovered.

Since at one time the parents had had to forgive, they take it for granted that their children will likewise forgive them everything. They regard this as their right, and the children feel guilty, bad, and damned if they go to bed at night bearing a grudge against their parents. Since in past generations this fundamental experience was familiar to almost everybody, it is only natural that therapists throughout the world should insist that their patients forgive. I have demonstrated the disadvantages of this insistence in *Thou Shalt Not Be Aware,* but meanwhile I have become even better acquainted with the *dangers* of this attitude. As long as psychoanalysis dominated the field of therapy and did not allow patients even to approach their feelings, pedagogic demands were perhaps not always threatening because they did not go beyond an intellectual and hence nonbinding scope. But as modern forms of therapy developed, the patients' blocked feelings were awakened and energies were set free. However, the patients could not be truly accompanied in these feelings, nor could they resolve them, as long as the moral basis for such therapies was the demand that, after every temporarily sanctioned outburst of anger, they forgive their parents unconditionally.

I was told of a man who, after the conclusion of such therapy, finally "forgave" his sadistic father "everything" and two years later, without the slightest warning, killed an innocent man. This report confirmed my assumption: When the capacity to feel has been achieved in therapy, the patient will become not less but more aware of events in his childhood that were never allowed to be

consciously experienced. Through the increasing famil-
iarity with his own feelings and his own history, it is
possible for a new memory to emerge years later, a memory to which at the time of intensive therapy there was as
yet no access. If a person is not allowed to acknowledge
the newly awakening anger—because, of course, he has
already forgiven his parents during therapy—the person
is in danger of transferring these feelings to others.
Since, to me, therapy means a sensory, emotional, and
mental discovery of the long-repressed truth, *I regard the
moral demand for reconciliation with parents as an inevitable
blocking and paralyzing of the therapeutic process.*

From readers' letters and verbal accounts, I have put
together a list of pedagogic pronouncements to be seen
as therapeutic interventions. They come from readers,
some of whom spent fifteen to twenty years in analysis,
who now find themselves in great distress and have asked
me for addresses of "nonpedagogic psychoanalysts."
The tragedy is that they do this despite my frequently
expressed opinion that *psychoanalysis per se* has never pro-
gressed beyond the pedagogic mentality. Very often the
reports contain comments by analysts such as the following:

- I am sure that was hard for you, but then it's so long
  ago. Isn't it time to forget?
- Your hatred isn't good for you; it poisons your life and
  prolongs your dependence on your parents. Only
  when you become reconciled with your parents will
  you be free of them.
- Try to see the positive aspects too: Didn't the parents
  whom you now call bad pay for your studies? Aren't
  you being unfair?

- I don't want to force you to forgive, but you will find no peace if you are so adamant, if you haven't forgiven.
- One can't get well as long as one blames other people; one must see the responsibility of the child too.
- The child is not a victim but a partner in an interaction.
- Your father used to be too strict with you *because* he was under a strain or *because* he was already ill; but he meant well and he loved you.
- Without punishment or withholding or setting limits, a child cannot learn the necessary norms; he would be unstable, even demoralized.
- Parents are human, too; they can't be perfect.

This list is only partial; it could be extended indefinitely. Common to all these remarks is that they are misleading and untrue yet are generally regarded as true because they have been around for so long. The child had to believe that the cruelties he suffered were for his own good, and later as an adult he will often be unable to recognize the untruth for what it is, especially if he is misled by people whom he finds quite likable, who arouse expectations in him, and who speak the same pedagogic language to which he has been accustomed from earliest childhood. For it has been proved to be *not* true that traumas occurring in the distant past do not torment a person. The process of forgetting helps the child to survive but not the adult patient to resolve his sufferings. The child *is* a defenseless victim, not an equal partner in interactions. Repressed, unconscious hatred has a destructive effect, whereas *relived* hatred is not a poison but one of the ways out of the trap of pretense, deceit, or overt destructiveness. And the patient really does get well when he stops sparing the aggressors by harboring guilt feelings, when he finally dares to see and feel what they have done.

The lengths to which the child's insistence on self-accusation can go are shown by the following example: A recognized and valued member of a sect, a man of forty, beat his two-year-old son for an hour because the son refused to say "I'm sorry." Asked later whether he hadn't noticed that the child, who was bleeding profusely, had already been dead for some time, he replied that he couldn't have stopped until the child apologized, since a child has to learn to say "I'm sorry" when he appears before God. What this father had learned as a child from his parents was incomparably more effective than the sight of his dying child.

The more I realized that many of today's therapists are protecting the childrearing system of their parents at the expense of their patients, the more did my mistrust of therapies increase and the more did my hope dwindle of one day finding a full confirmation of what I had recognized as true.

Then I came across Mariella Mehr's book *Steinzeit* (Stone Age), and it immediately gripped my attention. This woman was capable of tracking down very early experiences, reliving them, and enduring the truth, and she wrote a book without empty pedagogic phrases, without lies or retouching, without traditional morality, and with the knowledge of the monstrous truth of her childhood. Having just completed my manuscript of *Thou Shalt Not Be Aware,* I devoted the last two pages to the therapy undergone by Mariella Mehr. Later I asked her for the name of her therapist, J. Konrad Stettbacher, and got in touch with him. He explained his method to me, and I decided to test his procedures on myself, since his concept embraced everything that during the last few years I had found to be true.

Almost a hundred years ago, Sigmund Freud discovered in the symptoms of his female and male patients consequences of repressed childhood traumas and then renounced that discovery. Fifty years later, Sandor Ferenczi encountered the same phenomenon but died before he could construct a therapy method based on this insight. Another thirty years later, Robert Fliess arrived at a similar conclusion, again without developing a therapy method before he died: The fact is that both Ferenczi and Fliess remained locked in the prison of psychoanalytic concepts. Although they succeeded in flinging open a window of this prison and looking out, and although they succeeded in perceiving the situation of the abused child in their patients, they did not succeed in breaking out of their own prison of intellectual resistance and in developing a useful therapy concept.

Some eighty years after Freud's discovery, Arthur Janov observed in his patients that the experiencing of once-blocked pain led to the elimination of repression and to an awareness of early traumas, which brought about an astonishing improvement in symptomatology. This mere experiencing of primal feelings was called primal therapy by Janov even before he ever described a treatment concept or ever explained how the reader or the sufferer can set about experiencing his blocked pain. At times one gained the impression that those seeking help had to submit to a kind of rape *by* the therapist. Practice has also shown that pain induced under such circumstances, while providing some relief, was not sufficient to dissolve the destructive and self-destructive thought and behavior patterns.

157

It was the Swiss psychotherapist J. Konrad Stettbacher who succeeded in solving this problem. The explanation must be that, unlike Freud, Janov, and so many others, he was not satisfied with treating, observing, and describing patients. Instead, he wished to experience in himself his new method of gaining access to his traumas and consistently applied those methods over many years.

It was this personal access that opened his eyes to the extent of destruction inflicted on a child out of ignorance. Not until we begin to perceive this destruction with the sensory powers of a child, with the knowledge of a victim, can we rid ourselves of the unconscious identification with the destructive actions of parents and thus break the chain of repetition. Because only then do we dare condemn those actions unreservedly. The mere observing of patients, however honest and well intentioned it may be, does not protect us from still applying pedagogic patterns to patients, without being aware of it. If we have not consciously felt the effect of these patterns in ourselves, we continue, like Freud and many of his famous successors who never went beyond the intellectual study of childhood, to be at the mercy of these patterns. I have experienced this innumerable times in myself and with others.

Apart from Stettbacher's recently published book, I know of no systematic description of primal therapy. When I visited the Institute for Primal Therapy in Paris in 1985 I addressed Janov on this subject. He accounted for the lack of a concept in his books by his concern that this form of treatment might be misused, and he considered only those students licensed by him as qualified to perform it. Yet in my view it is hardly possible to protect a method by authoritarian measures. Rather, a precise,

responsible description, one that gives readers some orientation, can protect potential patients and therapists
from misuse and help them avoid the dangers of a pedagogic therapist who doesn't know what he is doing.

The lack of a verifiable concept of primal therapy
turned out to be a great disadvantage to patients because
it failed to prevent chaotic, dangerous experimentation
but instead encouraged it. Access to primal pain, and the
possibility of dissolving it through the perception of
one's own needs, must also be precisely described for the
sake of the autonomy of the person seeking help. But,
above all, this access is unlikely to be found spontaneously, without guidance, since in each person there exists a strong resistance to stressful primal experiences.
The patient as well as future therapists can learn from
such guidance how to overcome this resistance step by
step instead of breaking it by force.

In my psychoanalytic training there was much discussion of the phenomenon of transference, and my own
practice confirmed its significance. Again and again I felt
that a person's need and ability to transfer long-repressed emotions to subsequent reference persons contain a high therapeutic potential of which psychoanalysis
has never become fully aware. It is true, though, that
transference phenomena were extensively misused to
promote the analyst's exertion of power and the incapac-
ity of patients.

Sigmund Freud himself, as well as thousands of his
successors, *explained* to their patients why those patients
were doing, saying, feeling this or that, why they hated,
desired, loathed, or envied the analysts. And the analysts
were convinced that they really knew the answers. Although their explanations were derived from learned

theories, constructs, and their own educational background, and often had nothing whatever to do with the
factual life of their patients, the patients believed their
analysts' every word, as the faithful do their priests'.
They didn't know that they should have had both the
right and the chance to be accompanied on the journey
to their feelings so that they could find the *correct* explanation for their feelings on their own.

For when it is no longer a matter of demonstrating a
patient's allegedly innate destructive tendencies by
means of transference; when, on the contrary, the aim is
to allow the patient to feel which were the concrete
events that have sent him into a rage so that he can
articulate that rage with all its relative facets, then entirely new, undreamed of possibilities open up for using
this so-called transference for therapeutic purposes.

It is rare for the patient to perceive and feel the misery
of his childhood by way of direct memories. These memories are either completely banished, a prey to amnesia,
or separated from feelings, emotionally inaccessible, and
hence of little help. But the real history is betrayed by the
behavior of the patient toward current reference persons, even toward those of secondary significance.

Stettbacher shows in his therapy how these lesser and
greater everyday transferences can be systematically uti-
lized for therapeutic purposes. Since the history of unresolved early traumas tends to be told and eventually
heard, it appears in ever-new "editions." It appears as a
result of individual promptings—in coded form, to be
sure, but with astonishing precision. The code can be
deciphered if the various new "editions" can be experienced with the relevant feelings. In this process the therapist need not even be the main object of the transfer-

ence, for *he is not alone* in controlling the work, as he would be in analysis. The patient's increasing autonomy enables him, thanks to the tools he has been given, to supervise and resolve his transferences. He is capable at any time of taking up the emerging feelings with the current reference person, of confronting him inwardly, of challenging him, and of communicating his needs to him.

It can but need not happen that the therapist, through his attitude, releases feelings in the patient that the patient must take up. Like anyone else, the therapist can evoke the memory of past events. But the therapist is not the only person around whom the patient's feelings constantly revolve, as they do in psychoanalysis. He accompanies the patient and helps him to find his way among his newly awakened feelings, to endure his fears and articulate his needs. At times he will have to protect the once abused child from killing himself or others as a result of the old despair, now for the first time consciously experienced. Thus the role of transference is less pronounced in Stettbacher's primal therapy than in psychoanalysis—as far as the person of the therapist is concerned. But the therapeutic yield of this phenomenon is incomparably greater, wider, and more precise than was ever the case throughout the whole history of psychoanalysis. Moreover, this phenomenon is placed entirely at the disposal of the patient, who can apply it as a means of self-help. He can use his transferred feelings to deepen his self-recognition, and he need not be ashamed of them.

Stettbacher's therapy avoids the danger of misuse by its transparency. Moreover, on the surface it is not attractive enough to tempt prestige-seeking therapists to be trained in it. It does not entice with an exclusive group membership that promises social power. All it does is consistently offer patients the truth, that is, the opportunity to encounter their own past that they have been trying to escape at all costs. Its tools are theoretically verifiable, it harbors no secrets, and for purposes of self-help it can be learned and tested in practice by anyone with a will to get to know his childhood. According to his situation and his potential, anyone can apply it creatively. There are no dictates and no rituals that guarantee power to the therapist and that must be complied with. There are only the clear lines of goal setting and the means to do so. The set goal is the recognition of one's own injuries (abuse and neglect) suffered in childhood. This is achieved by experiencing and resolving primal pain and by becoming liberated from latent destructive and self-destructive reactions. Access to primal experiences leads from current "promptings" to concrete inner confrontations. The resolving takes place by means of the four steps that I illustrate with an example in Chapter 3 of Part II. Of course, one of the requirements of the therapy is that there be a person both accessible and approachable who can assume the role of the missing enlightened witness. That is the basic outline: no mystification, no archetypes, no spirits, no magic, no gurus, only the painful journey to the facts, to the relinquishing of blindness, illusions, and the useless prostheses of self-delusion and confusion. The reward for these efforts is nothing less than a great relief provided by clarity: That's how it was, I can stop pretending, stop letting myself be confused, stop suppressing my knowledge; I'm free to see, live, breathe, recount, and I can no longer be prevented from knowing the truth and expressing it.

J. Konrad Stettbacher's therapy will without a doubt offer the appropriate tools to those who are looking for their reality rather than illusions. This concept has helped me to advance from the vague suppositions and assumptions that I gleaned from my spontaneous painting, to the unequivocal facts, and to repeated tests of those facts with the aid of my feelings and inner confrontations. Some of my discoveries were confirmed, others turned out to be acts of embellishment necessary for survival. However, a great deal appeared in a new, unexpected light; for even my painting was concerned only with symbolic content. It was a vague intimation of what was hidden in the unconscious and gave me no certainty about actual occurrences as long as my instilled guilt feelings kept giving rise to new doubts so as to idealize my parents. It was only the constant querying and testing of my hypotheses that gave those intimations a firm foundation and clear contours.

This process of deepening one's insights is never fully terminated, nor need it be. But today I can afford, to a far greater extent than ever before, to know what happened to me in my childhood. I owe a lot to this knowledge: I am now free of physical symptoms, some of which I had suffered since childhood, and I have lost the fears that have also accompanied me all my life.

After spending four years applying J. Konrad Stettbacher's carefully thought-out method to myself, I see ever more clearly that it amounts to the discovery of an inherent logical pattern in human beings, the functioning of which anyone can test. As distinct from psychoanalysis, whose theories are still based entirely on the pedagogic view of innocent parents, and from all other forms of therapy known to me, in which pedagogy still reigns unquestioned, Stettbacher's concept contains no trace of pedagogy. Its aim is to uncover the individual's reality from beneath the detritus of old injuries. For this it is necessary that these injuries be recognized and that, with the aid of present feelings, they be found and, furthermore, that it no longer be permissible for anyone to be spared when it comes to discovering the truth, since it was lies that hindered the child from living and seeing. It is also necessary that the previously injured child learn in therapy to make use of the potential with which nature has richly endowed him and of which he was robbed by adults, that he learn to experience and articulate feelings, to challenge encroachments and accusations and to repulse them, and finally to be aware of his own needs and to look for opportunities of fulfilling them.

Essentially, a world of possibilities opens up to a person as soon as he no longer needs to evade the truth, but the fear of pain and the associated blockages have long barred his access to this world. Every genuine need is overlaid with fear and leads to severe tension and self-punishment instead of fulfillment so long as stored memories tell only of punishment rather than fulfillment.

Such was also my own case. My mother saw my natural needs as tiresome demands. How could I, sent out into the world thus equipped, have had any inkling of what I really needed? How could I have learned to satisfy those needs? I learned that they were dangerous because the desire for satisfaction inevitably led to disaster. That disaster, the great threat, was my mother's rage and my exposure to her lack of love. So I tried with all my might to suppress my needs for affection, warmth, and understanding to avoid having to see how my mother really felt about me and to maintain the illusion of her love. My hope was that if I needed nothing and sacrificed my life for others, surely I would eventually be given that love. But love cannot be earned, whether by self-denial or by altruistic service. It is either given at birth, or it isn't. I finally had to acknowledge that I had not received this gift as a child.

That sounds very simple, but for almost sixty years I didn't dare *feel* this reality, although I was intellectually aware of it. Not until I could feel it, together with all the associated memories, did the buried possibilities of my life open up to me—at least those that had not been irreparably destroyed.

If this path was still open to me even at my age, it is certainly accessible to a younger person, provided that she actually *wants* to confront her history of suffering and is not satisfied with finding substitute culprits. In the latter case, patients will presumably cut short their primal therapy. They may perhaps join sects and continue to direct their feelings of rage and indignation against substitute persons. They will blame all kinds of people, including the therapist, to spare at all costs the true authors of their injuries, the parents of their early childhood, and, tragically, will remain fixated on them.

Thanks to its precision, Stettbacher's therapy offers a chance to track down the specific causes of those injuries and to carefully test accepted intellectual opinions and hypotheses on the subject of parents in concrete terms. But this can hardly be done without pain. If this pain cannot be endured because the emerging memories of actual abuse are so unbearable, one can understand that some patients abandon this treatment and remain locked

165

in their self-destructive fixations. However, for those who are able, and want, to feel the *specific* truth, the pain and fear on which they were fixated on account of their injuries and which were a lifelong obstacle to living will dissolve.

This liberation from old fears has opened my eyes to many things: to the mute signals of the child, to the hidden mechanisms of society that destroy the soul of the child, and to the chance of saving children and thus our future through enlightened witnesses.

TWO

THE ENLIGHTENED
WITNESS

A PROFESSOR of philosophy in the United States wrote
to me several years ago along the following lines:

I have read your three books and for the first time understand
why my two analyses were failures. Since then, in my search for
an expert who is familiar with your books and has integrated
them into his work, I have interviewed a number of therapists,
some of them from among our acquaintances. Although they
all knew your name and apparently had read *The Drama of the
Gifted Child,* I was surprised to find that they all used the same
vocabulary in discussing your ideas, as if they had all met and

An abbreviated version of this chapter in a different translation appeared in
the journal *Mothering*, New Mexico (Summer 1987).

167

agreed on how these ideas were to be assessed. Yet these were people who scarcely knew one another. They declared unanimously that you say nothing in your books that other analysts, such as Kohut and Winnicott, for example, have not already said, but that in your simplification you have gone "much too far."

When I protested and tried to explain that it wasn't until I read your books that I became aware of my reality, I met with an unyielding and similarly uniform rejection. On my raising specific questions from *Thou Shalt Not Be Aware*, I discovered that most of those therapists, while owning your books, hadn't found time to read them. They kept referring to your narcissism theory, which you have never mentioned again since *Drama*, and they suggested that your chief merit was that you had introduced psychoanalysis to the public. I was invariably annoyed to find myself so intimidated by the self-assurance of each therapist in turn that only when I got home did I think of rebuttals, although I had read all your books several times.

There was one therapist who seemed less rigid and arrogant, and with him I did try, timidly, to formulate my point of view. I began with a purely logical argumentation and demonstrated that one can't tell the same author that her discovery has long since been known and at the same time claim that her statements are wrong: either it is a discovery or it isn't. I received no reply, as if this were no longer of any consequence whatever. The young man behind his desk suddenly looked at me with wide eyes and said: "But Alice Miller blames the parents!" "So?" I asked. Again no reply, but at that moment I didn't dare ask any more questions. I felt I could sense his fear, and I wanted to respect it.

Is it possible that this fear explains why I cannot find a therapist to accompany me? We've all had parents, after all. Why is it that therapists and analysts of all people benefit less from your books than everybody else? They react with annoyance to the mere mention of child abuse and are obviously afraid of casting doubt on parents. How can they support me when I feel that the path I must take is the very one they are afraid of?

The conversations usually ended in my being advised to seek therapy from one of your "followers." But I am not looking for followers, I am looking for a therapist who does not evade the questions you ask, because these are also my questions and because I also find them again in the evasive attitude of the therapists.

I have received a great many similar letters, with many personal details, most of them ending with a request for therapists who might have integrated my work into their own. The foregoing letter shows why I cannot fulfill these requests. But it also shows that the critical faculty of patients is growing and that this growing critical faculty will one day help patients to distinguish the real from the supposed support.

In *Thou Shalt Not Be Aware* I have in several places mentioned criteria that searching patients can use as guidelines. However, each patient must examine to what extent the person offering his help can bear the truth and to what extent he is suited to accompany and support a formerly abused child in his search for the truth.

When I say that many people find it difficult to understand my books, I often meet with astonishment, and some say: How can anyone not understand your books? You stick to facts that we are all familiar with from everyday life and that we can check out. You have cleared away the theoretical ballast that obscures the sight of the truth. The reaction of many people to your books is: How true! How can anyone *not* understand them?

This question was also put to me by the well-known anthropologist Ashley Montagu. For him, my books are clear and explicit because, thanks to his research in various cultures, he also discovered, many decades ago, that the child is not wicked at birth but is brought up by his environment to be a wicked person. Most people don't know this because they aren't allowed to know. And such people are bound to misunderstand my books. Since earliest childhood they have learned that they must take the blame for everything done to them by their environment, and by the time they are students they have come to take for granted the theories on the innate destructiveness of human beings. They believe in this because these teachings were stored in them at an early age, and the university cements these teachings with the customary socially conforming theories.

So when these people read my books they are given a chance to query what they were taught as children and later at university as students. But this chance is all that I can give them. How they make use of it will depend mainly on whether in their childhood they were sufficiently at liberty to query their parents' behavior and opinions or whether this was totally forbidden because the parents had to be regarded as infallible, blameless persons. In the latter case, the doors to any later questioning of the parents and of instilled opinions sometimes remain closed forever, and the learning capacity of such people is severely handicapped. As a result, they pass on to their own children their parents' pernicious ideas of disciplining and childrearing, without the slightest misgivings. If I as a helpless child was abused and *am not allowed to see this,* I will abuse other helpless creatures without realizing what I am doing. I will also refuse to read books by Alice Miller, or I won't *want* to understand them because, if I did, I would have to feel the tragedy of my childhood and the pain of having been misled at such an early age.

There is no other, easier path. Once someone has read and understood my books, he can no longer remain insensitive toward the child, neither his own child nor himself. But this awakening of sensitivity for the martyrdom of childhood has far-reaching consequences: Suddenly it is no longer possible to regard cruelty, perversion, and crime as a form of upbringing for our own good; we are forced to come to a decision and stop finding excuses for crime.

Some people can already do this. They want to stop contributing to the covering up of the truth. They work with abused children; they see what is being done to children every day; they see how state, school, and the children themselves are protecting crimes without recognizing them as such. Who are these few people? Even if they, like the rest of us, had to endure "poisonous pedagogy," they must in their childhood have encountered at least *one* person who was not cruel to them, who thus enabled them to become aware of their parents' cruelty. For this awareness, a supporting and hence corrective witness is required. A child who knows nothing but cruelty and who lacks such a witness will never recognize it as such.

What I have said so far sounds very pessimistic because it accounts for people's ignorance—the great threat to the future of humanity—by the atrophy of their emotional learning capacity in childhood. Of what use is writing, speaking, imparting knowledge, one might think, when so many people cannot help but remain blind?

I believe that this can change, that something will

change in the very next generation if we cease to expose our children to the abuse known as discipline and child-rearing. Children who have grown up respected run no risk in telling their parents if they happen to feel they are being cruelly treated by them. Yet for many adults of the present generation this was absolutely unthinkable when they were children. Formerly abused children could never say, "How dreadful my childhood was!" Instead they said, "That's life, that's normal. That's how I'll bring up my own children too. After all, I've turned out all right." The early destruction of their learning capacity bears late fruit.

Must we wash our hands of these adults? Is it too late to help them with information because as children they were programmed not to be aware of the cruelty inflicted on them and, consequently, of any child abuse? I don't think so. My hope is linked to my concept of the enlightened witness. If I succeed with my books in reaching a few people who were fortunate enough to have had a helpful witness in their childhood, even if only for a short time, then, after reading my books, they will become enlightened, *conscious* witnesses and advocates of children. Wherever they live, they will become aware of the suffering of children more quickly and more deeply than others who must deny it. They will try to uncover the child abuse that occurs unconsciously and is taken for granted by others. In doing so, they will change public awareness, and even the most relentless supporters of punishment will be forced to notice that much of what they had so far regarded as right and proper is life-destroying. Let me cite an example described to me by a child psychotherapist from Northern California.

A girl had told the therapist that in school the children

were locked up in small, windowless rooms when they disrupted the class. He wrote a report on this and was dismissed from his job as school counselor. After making a thorough study of various cases he found that this system of punishment was practiced in other schools too. A number of articles appeared concerning the case, and for the first time those involved realized that this was a matter of child abuse. I telephoned the psychologist to congratulate him on his courage and to assure him of my solidarity, because I know how one's self-confidence can be shaken, how isolated a person can feel, when he knows he is in the right yet everyone else is against him. In an environment in which everyone agrees that a child can learn something good by being punished, a person's first reaction is that he is wrong in maintaining the opposite. For, after all, the words of his own parents are still ringing in his ears, the parents in whom he once had as much faith as if they were gods. Doubts begin to arise: Is it possible that I am wrong if not a single person among so many is prepared to share the child's perspective? Yet it is possible that all those others are wrong.

Interventions like the one I just described are not a drop in the ocean: Their effectiveness is very great. The press picks up the incident, with the result that many people are confronted with questions that they had hitherto evaded, among others the following: What are the feelings of a child who has been locked up as a punishment? What happens to his soul when, to be reinstated in the community, to please the teacher, he must repress the feelings of impotence and despair generated by that teacher? What has he learned from this punishment other than to dissemble and, later, as an adult, likewise to resort to violence and to avenge himself on children?

173

People who were not warped while at university are much more open to such questions. In the course of conversation with a cab driver in London, an East Indian, I asked whether he beat his children. He said he had never beaten his daughter, only his son, because the boy must, after all, grow up to be "a man of character" and this could be accomplished only by punishment. I asked him whether he had been beaten too, and he said he had. I asked whether he remembered what he had learned from being punished. He didn't. Then he suddenly said: "Or do you believe a man beats his own child only because he was beaten himself?"

That's how simple it is to achieve an insight if one hasn't spent years, and considerable time and money, studying the reverse at schools and universities with no opportunity to gain new experience with healthy children. But we are moving in the right direction, and what children who were never tormented can tell us is so unambiguous that it should help us see through the lies of the established theories. People who from earliest childhood have been taken seriously, have been respected, loved, and protected, cannot but treat their own children in the same way because their souls and their bodies have absorbed and stored this lesson at an early age. From the very beginning they learned that it is right to protect and respect the weaker, and it becomes something they take for granted. They will need no psychology textbooks to raise their children. But people who determine the lives of children today—parents, teachers, jurists—had different experiences in their childhood, and they still believe those were correct. They can seldom empathize with children or summon up any feeling for their own childhood fate. Only with the emergence of conscious witnesses and children's advocates will their certainty vanish. Eventually they will have to abandon those mistaken theories and learn from experience if they don't want to be overtaken by other contemporaries. I believe that we are on the way to achieving this goal because in the future, thanks to new insights, more and more people will have had a humane childhood. Daniel's history, told in the next chapter, shows the reasons for my hopes.

THREE

THE CHILD SETS LIMITS

ON THE BASIS of the pedagogy that was practiced on us, the exerting of unlimited power by the adult over the child is still taken for granted. Most people know nothing else. It is only from a child who was never injured that we can learn entirely new, honest, and truly humane behavior. Such a child does not accept without question the pedagogic reasoning to which we were susceptible. He feels he is entitled to ask questions, to demand explanations, to stand up for himself, and to articulate his needs. A young woman from the United States related to me the following incident:

176

I once took my three-year-old Daniel to stay with my mother for two days, not without some misgivings for I knew that my mother had been a great one for discipline and attached great importance to good manners. On the other hand she was very fond of Daniel, and he of her because when she came to stay with us she liked to read him stories. However, when I picked him up after those two days he said to me in the car: "I don't want to stay with Grandma anymore." Astonished, I asked him why, and he replied: "She hurt me."

When I phoned my mother to ask what had happened, she told me that Daniel had cried when she tried to explain to him at table that a well-brought-up little boy mustn't go ahead and help himself without saying "please" and "thank you." My mother felt I was spoiling Daniel and teaching him very bad manners. She felt obliged to correct this so that later on the child wouldn't annoy people and be treated with contempt and dislike, instead of love, from those around him. She was convinced she was trying to help him and wasn't aware that she was under a compulsion originating in her childhood fear. She didn't realize that she was threatening the child with a withdrawal of love if he didn't obey. And above all she didn't realize, as she hadn't in my own case, that she was sacrificing the child's soul to empty conventions just as had been done to her sixty years earlier.

But Daniel realized it. He couldn't have put it into words, not in the way I do now, but he expressed it in the way that was possible to *him*, as I found out from the exact description of the facts that gradually evolved from my mother's account. The story was perfectly simple: The dessert was Daniel's favorite, cottage-cheese soufflé. When he had finished the helping he had been given, he picked up the serving spoon and reached out to help himself to some more. He always does this at home, taking great pride in his independence. But now my mother held him back, gently placing her hand, as she told me, on his and saying: "You must first ask whether you may have some

177

and whether there is enough for others." "Where are the others?" asked Daniel, and began to cry. He threw down the spoon and refused to eat any more, although my mother urged him to: he said he wasn't hungry anymore and wanted to go home. My mother tried to calm him, but he threw a real tantrum. After a few minutes his rage was spent, and he said: "You hurt me, I don't like you. I want to go to Mommy." After a while he asked: "Why did you do that? I know how to help myself." "Yes," said my mother, "but you must first ask whether you may." "Why?" asked Daniel. "Because you must learn good manners." "What for?" asked Daniel. "Because one needs them," replied my mother. Daniel then said quite calmly: "*I* don't need them. With Mommy I can eat when I'm hungry."

That is the reaction of a healthy three-year-old if he had learned at home that it is all right to stand up for himself, that he is entitled to be given food by his parents because they obviously owe it to him, since they decided to have a child. This child is allowed to defend himself, to show his anger, when his natural gesture is impeded and he is given a reason that he doesn't understand, can't understand, and shouldn't understand, because it is senseless and really only comprehensible in terms of his grandmother's history. When a small child observes that the grown-ups at table say Please and Thank you, he will automatically do the same without having to be taught. That such an attempt to train him made Daniel furious is easy enough to understand. He had a chance to voice his anger because he could compare his grandmother's attempt at training him with the happy experience he had with his parents.

I wasn't given this chance. I remembered, but only recently, that my mother drilled such things into me every day without my ever being able to protest. How could I have dared? I was absolutely at her mercy. I couldn't say, "If you treat me like this I want to go home to Mommy," for *she* was my mother. In fact, I couldn't even be aware of what she was doing because I knew nothing else. From this little episode about Daniel I understood yet again that the tragedy of my childhood lay not only in my being constantly at the mercy of my mother's pedagogic devices, not only in my being afraid to offer resistance, but above all in the *impossibility of my realizing what was happening.* When I entitled my books *For Your Own Good* and *Thou Shalt Not Be Aware,* little did I know how much of my own history was embraced by these titles.

For the three-year-old boy, and presumably for many other children who today are growing up in greater freedom, it was possible to take the "four steps" that are an essential ingredient of the Stettbacher therapy: (1) *describing the situation and one's sensations;* (2) *experiencing and expressing emotions;* (3) *querying the situation;* and (4) *articulating needs.* Since this sequence follows a natural pattern of healthy human self-defense and self-protection, one might wonder why this pattern remained undiscovered for so long. It is in the nature of child injuries that they destroy this natural, innate capacity. So the possibility of taking the four steps must be rediscovered in therapy so that the vague history of childhood, with all its crass and subtle abuses, acquire clear contours in the adult's consciousness and cease to block him with guilt feelings.

Daniel appeared to be free of this blockage. Had he not known positive experiences with his parents, the lightest touch of his grandmother's hand to prevent him from serving himself would presumably have made him

179

feel ashamed. He would have been ashamed of having done something wrong, of not having good manners; he might even have been ashamed of his pride in his independence. For apparently this was the very thing that was not acceptable—at least not at the moment when he wanted to help himself to some food, in other words, to do something of immense importance to himself. He was held back, made to feel unsure of himself. Had he grown up with a pedagogic background, he would have stored this lesson forever in his brain and his limbs: I mustn't enjoy my food, I mustn't satisfy my healthy appetite, even when there's enough food. I must first do things I don't understand, I must submit to an incomprehensible law that takes away my appetite, puts me under stress, and gives me feelings of guilt and shame, a law in whose hands I am totally powerless. Depending on later development, the result can be lifelong digestive troubles and a variety of eating compulsions and cravings that lead to anorexia or bulimia.

I don't wish by this example to imply that a person will become ill if he has experienced such a situation only once. After all, we have seen how three-year-old Daniel managed to avoid being harmed by it. This is not a severe traumatic experience and presumably will leave no mark on Daniel, who was able to stand up for himself. However, had he not been the grandson of this woman but her own child, he would have had no choice but to submit to these manipulations known as childrearing and to develop, in addition to eating disorders, various other inhibitions to self-awareness.

FOUR

WHY I REJECT PSYCHOANALYSIS ALSO AS A THERAPY METHOD

FOLLOWING MY INTERVIEW for the April 1987 issue of the German journal *Psychologie heute* (Psychology Today), in which I declared my break with psychoanalysis, I was asked several times whether I didn't owe psychoanalysis the means that enabled me to query it. Today I can answer this question with a clear No. As recently as in my preface to the first German edition of *Thou Shalt Not Be Aware*, I succumbed to this error myself. Yet later developments showed me unmistakably that psychoanalysis is a maze from which it is very difficult to find a way out. Without the illusionary help of psychoanalysis, which furthers the resistance to knowledge about past events, there is no doubt that I would have found my way to the truth sooner.

I owe my first awakening to the spontaneous pictures that I began to paint in 1973. Nevertheless, even years later, in 1981, I still closed my eyes to the fact that psychoanalysis was the very thing that had kept me away from feelings blocked since my childhood and thus from the truth. I didn't discover this until, thanks to J. Konrad Stettbacher's method, I could approach my childhood step by step.

What I find most convincing about this method is its openness to creativity, its precision, its effectiveness, its verifiability, and its respect for the uniqueness and special quality of each individual life and history. Since it makes the path to reality possible and is not afraid of reality, it is free of lies, of being enmeshed in any way with them, free of clichés, pedagogy, moralizing norms, spiritual mystifications, and any and all associated ideological trimmings.

On the other hand, there is proof that these elements are present in psychoanalysis, and I have supplied such proofs in my earlier books. Today I realize: It was an illusion to believe that the remains of pedagogy could be removed from psychoanalysis, leaving it still suitable for the liberation of those seeking help. It is no coincidence that psychoanalysis has not yet undertaken any revision of its immanent pedagogy; it cannot do this, for as soon as the pedagogic scaffolding is removed the whole structure will collapse like a house of cards. Since in the past psychoanalysis has served only to disguise childhood traumas, how can it now be expected to help abused children? This inability is revealed not only in its theory but also in every detail of its technique—which is useless for getting at the truth.

Even if some analysts do wish not to manipulate their patients according to theories and pedagogic morality, but wish instead to accompany them in the discovery of their history, they are bound to fail as long as they work with the method of free association. This method, also known as a basic rule, reinforces intellectual resistance to feelings and reality; for as long as feelings can be talked *about* they cannot really be felt. And as long as feelings are not felt, the self-damaging blockages remain.

Both basic rules—the psychoanalytic setting as well as the method of free association—assume that on the one side there is a superior, informed interpreter, the analyst, and on the other the uninformed patient to whom the analyst explains his situation, his unconscious desires, thoughts, and impulses. For the analyst to be able to do this, the patient must as it were uncover, betray, and expose his unconscious with the aid of free association. Thus the authoritarian structure of child-rearing is preserved unthinkingly in both basic rules. Parents, too, told the child from *their* perspective how he felt, or how he was supposed to feel, and the child believed that they knew better than he did.

On the basis of this pedagogic model, indissolubly coupled as it is with Freudian constructs, the student analysands learn to discuss the patient's emotions and "to be in the know," but never to feel anything themselves. No wonder they in turn cannot enable anyone else to feel anything. The patient senses that inability and as a rule will not dare to admit any feelings. If he does, perhaps because he has read books that for the first time opened up some access to his pain, he will quickly learn in psychoanalytic practice to bring order into his suffering, to define it with abstract words, and to manipulate it so as to "feel better" again. He will sense that the interpreters of his soul feel threatened by emotions, because in their constructs they have learned only how to fend them off, and he will do anything to avoid exposing his substitute parents to this threat. He will adapt to their method of free association and talk to them about his feelings without realizing that he is letting himself in for years and years of wandering about in a maze, while in the meantime he is missing his chance of living. For his benumbed life cannot awaken until the child's confrontation with the authors of his suffering begins; until the patient ceases to philosophize and wonder why his parents did this or that to him and instead begins, with the aid of numerous transferences, to uncover *what* exactly they did do; until in therapy he can finally confront his internalized parents with his suffering; until with each new pain reminding him of the old one he tries to tell himself what he is feeling and then tests the situation. Just as Daniel did. That which the unharmed child can externalize with his reference persons in reality, the once harmed adult has to try out and learn within the protective setting of therapy. How this works in each case has been made clear in Stettbacher's description of his method.

It is not possible for someone really to clarify his situation and dissolve his fears until he can *feel* them rather than discuss them. Only then is the veil lifted and he realizes his true need: not a tutor, not an interpreter, not a confuser; he needs space for his own growth and the company of an enlightened witness on the long journey on which he has set out.

184

Someone who has himself never learned to feel will not know that he makes it impossible for the other person, the patient, to feel. It is enough, for instance, to explain to the patient the distress of his parents or of other people for all the patient's latent reproaches to be instantly silenced. He hasn't any, he isn't aware of any, all he feels is pity for the authors of his distress. For it is impossible to feel the pain and at the same time understand why it was inflicted. One simply does not feel it.

It took me years to get away from this "understanding" attitude. The habit, originating in psychoanalysis, of working with free associations proved to be the greatest obstacle in my own therapy. Time after time, free association enabled me to establish ingenious, intellectual links and thus obtain what I imagined was an overview. This helped me to evade the painful confrontation with my parents and in turn blocked all the avenues through which I might have gained some insight into the reality of my childhood. As long as I could put a name to my feelings, I retained mastery over the child in me, making it impossible for her to find her language, the language of hitherto unnamed sensations and feelings. The technique of the four steps helped me become aware of this blockage because I found that, significantly, I tended to skip the first two steps. Finally, after a long time, I could allow the child in me to express her sensations and feelings and to take her time in doing so. But she could feel only when the adult, educated part of me allowed this to happen and without the interference of explanations and associations.

This experience helped me to discover that Freud, with his method, created a system of self-deception that functioned reliably to promote repression. Anyone who does *not* want to know the truth about his life will find psychoanalysis helpful. In any case he will be helped to reinforce the old resistance to the injuries suffered in childhood and never to find out the truth about what happened.

Philosophers and other intellectuals have fashioned numerous ways of keeping pain at a distance with the aid of thoughts and of disregarding the realities of life with the aid of an ostensibly defining language. In fact, Martin Heidegger made this the goal of his philosophy. He touched on his former painful and denied experiences only with abstract thoughts that excluded any feelings of the child since the child would have recognized the self-deception. For him there was no duality of passion and thought but only passionate thought, which did not advance toward truth as a result of the thinking process but was itself the goal. It is said that, to make this clear, he once told his students, on introducing Aristotle: "Aristotle was born, worked, and died." In other words: It is only the philosopher's work that counts, not his life.

Until a few years ago I might have thought that Heidegger's error could be regarded as harmless and unimportant as long as his philosophy was not used to confuse the masses. But today I am no longer so sure, for recently I have received some proofs to the contrary—among other things, letters from several women philosophers writing to tell me that, through my books, they had for the first time grasped to what extent philosophy had kept them away from the truth. Its complicated thought processes had helped them not to see that they had been abused children. In spite of the suffering that now erupted, they were glad not to have completely missed the chance to live their lives, for they were still young enough to make use of it.

It is possible for a child to protect himself all through life from the tragic, unbearable truth by "passionate thinking" about "the nature of truth," and, as long as his symptoms do not sound the alarm, there the matter rests. However, psychoanalysis is a system that offers the very people who have symptoms an escape from their plight. That is why such people must be told that they can expect no solution in psychoanalysis. The most they can expect is a maze of well-tended paths but with no exit into freedom. It is a prison built with the theories of a man who a century ago found himself in the same quandary as most patients do today. To escape insight into the martyrdom of his childhood, he fled into the garden of thought constructs, and for a while his symptoms disappeared. But they came back despite increasing efforts to keep the artificial structure from collapsing.

Galileo went blind after being forced by the Church to repudiate the truth against his better knowledge. Sigmund Freud forbade himself to voice the truth he had discovered about child abuse and its effects on the psyche of the adult. He betrayed his own discovery after his father's death. When I read that he later suffered from cancer of the jaw and that after many operations he finally died of it, I have to ask myself whether his jaw was not rebelling on behalf of the truth on which he chose to turn his back. Although my question is to be regarded merely as a hypothesis which, in the absence of the person involved, I cannot put to the test, I have noticed that, among the innumerable analysts who are so fond of handing out interpretations to their dependent patients, not one of them, as far as I know, has yet published an interpretation of Freud's illness. Are the disciples not permitted even to wonder why a venerated father figure contracted cancer of the jaw? May interpretations be given only to dependent persons—children and patients? Doesn't this amount to admitting that interpretations are weapons used against the helpless but not against an authority held in awe? Patients are fed all kinds of constructs by the old man and believe that this is genuine nourishment. They believe everything because they need someone who will at last listen to them. And they do not see through the abuse because someone who in childhood experienced nothing but abuse is unable later in life to see through it.

The man who was no longer allowed to utter the truth instead wrote volume after volume whose style was universally admired and whose contents led humanity into utter confusion. So "passionate thinking" is by no means as harmless as it appears. In my opinion, everything that suppresses the truth is destructive, even if the consequences cannot be fully recognized until much later.

In my view, Stettbacher succeeded in finding a way to the injured child in the adult, letting that child express himself with the aid of feelings, and in conceptualizing this way of experiencing the past. This is not to say that there can be no other methods that, based on the same insight into early injuries, enable the same goal to be achieved. The efficacy of various methods will become apparent as soon as publications on the subject become available.

Yet one thing remains certain: Since the injured child in us can express himself only by means of physical sensations and feelings related to his traumas, it is essential that therapy secure access to these sensations and feelings and enable the person to articulate them. However, this access remains completely blocked whenever we are satisfied with intellectual speculations, as is the case in psychoanalysis. No matter how impressive and fashionable these speculations may be, they never go beyond the state of self-deception.

The invoking of great names such as Freud, Jung, Adler, and others as well as the application of their theories —theories that resist emotions and conceal the truth— cannot possibly help a therapist to rid a patient permanently of his neurosis. They will only produce new, emotion-resistant and ignorant "therapists" who cannot but remain ignorant as long as they cling to fictions, do not query what they once learned, are afraid of the truth, and wish to exert power.

The goal of therapy is to allow the once silenced child in us to speak and feel. Gradually the banishment of our knowledge is revoked, and in the course of this process, as the erstwhile torments and the still-existent prisons become evident, we also discover our history, ourself, and our buried capacity for love. A therapy of this kind can be carried out only by a therapist, female or male, who no longer keeps the child in himself and that child's knowledge in a state of banishment or who at least is moving in that direction—because he wants at all costs to find out the truth about himself.

APPENDIX

THE WAY OUT OF THE TRAP

NEWSPAPERS are constantly telling us that it has been proved statistically that most people who abuse their children were themselves abused in childhood. This information is not quite correct: It should be not "most" but all. Any person who abuses his children has himself been severely traumatized in his childhood in some form or another. This statement applies without exception since it is absolutely impossible for someone who has grown up in an environment of honesty, respect, and

The text of the article that the German journal refused to publish, as mentioned in Chapter Five, is printed here to serve as a summary of some of the thoughts in this book.

affection ever to feel driven to torment a weaker person in such a way as to inflict lifelong damage. He has learned very early on that it is right and proper to provide the small, helpless creature with protection and guidance; this knowledge, stored at that early stage in his mind and body, will remain effective for the rest of his life.

The foregoing applies without exception, although many people can scarcely remember the torments of their childhood because they have learned to regard them as a justified punishment for their own badness and also because a child must repress painful events in order to survive. This is why, in spite of new findings, sociologists, psychologists, and other experts continue to write that it is not known what leads to child abuse, and they speculate on the influence of cramped living conditions, unemployment, or the fear of nuclear war.

It is with such explanations that we protect the deeds of our parents. The fact is that there is no reason for child abuse other than the repression of the abuse and confusion once suffered by the abuser himself. The most cramped living conditions, the worst poverty, can never compel anyone to commit such a deed. Only those who are themselves victims of such deeds and allow them to remain repressed are in turn in danger of destroying other lives.

So-called difficult, "insufferable" children have been turned into such by adults. Not always by their own parents: Obstetrical and postpartum practices in many hospitals are often the first to contribute in large measure to this process. Some parents are able to compensate for these traumas by means of loving care, because they take them seriously and do not deny their danger. But parents who continue to repress their own severest traumas frequently tend, out of sheer ignorance, to downplay the importance of those traumas as applied to their own children, thus unnecessarily initiating a new chain of cruelty. Their insensitivity toward the child's suffering is fully supported by society, since most people, including the experts, share this blindness.

The sole means of preventing the spread of a disease is correct, well-documented information on its cause. Abusive parents need explicit information, being obscurely aware, as they are, that something is wrong when they vent their rage or satisfy their sexual urges on their defenseless child. Instead of taking this seriously, the experts beat about the bush for fear the parents might acquire guilt feelings, something which, so they misguidedly imagine, must under no circumstances occur.

This notion, that parents must never be blamed no matter what they have done, has caused untold damage. Let us look at reality. With the act of conception, parents enter on a commitment to care for the child, to protect him, to satisfy his needs, and not to abuse him. If they fail to fulfill this obligation, they actually remain in some degree indebted to the child, just as they would remain indebted to a bank after taking up a loan. They remain liable, regardless of whether or not they are aware of the consequences of their actions.

Is it permissible to bring a child into the world and ignore one's obligations? The child is not a toy or a kitten; he is a bundle of needs requiring a great deal of loving care to develop his potential. Those not prepared to give the child this must not have children. These words may sound harsh to people who have never experienced this loving care and so can never give it to their own children. For those who received protection and affection in their childhood and therefore were not starved, these words do not sound harsh. For them they are no more than truisms.

To beat a child, to humiliate him or sexually abuse him, is a crime because it damages a human being for life. It is important for third parties also to be aware of this, since enlightenment and the courage of witnesses can play a crucial, life-saving role for a child. The fact that every perpetrator was once a victim himself does not necessarily mean that each person who was himself abused is bound later to become the abuser of his own children. This is not inevitable if, during childhood, he had the chance—be it only once—to encounter someone who offered him something other than pedagogy and cruelty: a teacher, an aunt, a neighbor, a sister, a brother. It is only through the experience of being loved and cherished that the child can ever discern cruelty as such, be aware of it, and resist it. Without this experience he has no way of knowing that there is anything in the world except cruelty; the child will automatically submit to it and, years later, when as an adult he accedes to power, will exert it as being perfectly normal behavior.

Those who helped Hitler to carry out his schemes and to exterminate entire peoples must as children have had a similar experience to his: the constant presence of violence. Hence Hitler's attitude was something they took for granted. It was never questioned because throughout childhood apparently not a single person, not a single informed, enlightened witness, was available who might have intervened on the child's behalf. Such a witness might perhaps have helped the child to salvage his perceptive faculty and his character. To recognize cruelty, to reject it categorically, to be determined that one's own children never suffer it, the primary necessity is to be aware of its existence. Children strictly and cruelly brought up were not allowed to do that; they had to be grateful for the treatment they received from their parents, forgive them everything, always look for the cause of the outbursts in themselves, and under no circumstances were they permitted to call their parents' actions into question.

What happens when a child reared in love, protection, and honesty is suddenly beaten by someone? The child will scream, give vent to his anger, then burst into tears, reveal his pain, and probably ask: Why are you doing this to me? None of this is possible when a child trained from the very outset to be obedient is beaten by his own parents, whom he loves. The child must stifle his pain and anger and repress the whole situation to survive. For to be able to show anger the child needs the confidence based on experience that he will not be killed as a result. A battered child cannot build up this confidence; children are indeed sometimes killed when they dare to rebel against injustice. Hence the child must suppress his rage to survive in a hostile environment, must even stifle his massive, overwhelming pain in order not to die of it. So now the silence of forgetting descends over everything, and the parents are idealized—they have never done any wrong. "And if they did beat me, I deserved it." This is the familiar version of the torture that has been endured.

To forget and to repress would be a good solution if there were no more to it than that. But repressed pain blocks emotional life and leads to physical symptoms. And the worst thing is that, although the feelings of the abused child have been silenced at the point of origin, that is, in the presence of those who caused the pain, they find their voice when the battered child has children of his own. It is as if such people spent years and years caught in a trap from which there is no exit because anger directed at one's own parents is forbidden in our society. However, with the birth of one's own children a door opens: Here the pent-up rage of years can be ruthlessly discharged, unfortunately on a small, helpless creature that one has to torment, often without realizing it, driven to it by some unknown power.

The fact that parents often abuse or neglect their children in the same manner that they themselves were abused or neglected by their own parents, even if (and especially if!) they no longer have the slightest memory of those times, shows that they stored up their own traumas in their bodies. Otherwise they could not possibly reproduce them, which they do with amazing accuracy, an accuracy that comes to light as soon as they are prepared to feel their own helplessness instead of working it off on their own children and misusing their power.

How is a mother supposed to discover this truth on her own when society tells her in no uncertain terms that children must be disciplined and brought up to be decent members of society? Who cares that the driving force behind this disciplinary fervor is rage directed at her own mother, a rage that goes back many, many years and has never been experienced? Nor does the young woman want to know this. She thinks: It is my duty to discipline my child, and I do this in exactly or much the same way as my mother did to me. And after all, I've turned out all right, haven't I? I graduated with good marks, I've become involved in church work and the peace movement, and I've always spoken out against injustice. Only in the case of my own children I couldn't avoid having to beat them, though I really didn't want to; but there simply was no other way. I hope I haven't harmed them, just as it didn't do me any harm.

We are so used to such phrases that most people don't even notice them. But already there are some who do notice them, people who have decided to analyze the words of adults from the perspective of the child and are arriving at new knowledge, no longer afraid of letting in the light. They see that the destruction of a human life is not to be described as "ambivalent parental love" but must be recognized for what it is: a crime. Parents are not to be talked out of their guilt feelings; such feelings must be taken seriously. They are an indication that something has happened to the parents and that the parents need help. And they will seek this help when the only open door, which, tragically, leads to child abuse, is finally closed by a change in legislation. The parents will then be forced to look for another door: They will have to come to terms with their past to escape from their emotional trap without guilt.

Only when the child is no longer available as a legal scapegoat will this truly liberating process be open to the parents. An abusing father need not necessarily be punished by a prison term. It is possible, for instance, to imagine a court order stipulating that a father leave his family for a few months yet remain responsible for its support. If this father, suddenly left on his own, finds himself confronted with the feelings of his own childhood and at that point encounters an enlightened witness (possibly in the person of a knowledgeable social worker) who helps him to stop repressing that childhood situation, he is not likely to abuse his child after he returns. And the child will gain the significant, formative experience that he has grown up not in a jungle but in a humane society that truly respects his rights to protection and takes those rights seriously.

A prison term cannot bring about a change of heart. But therapists who, guided by the maxim "Help rather than punish," evade the truth are equally unable to change the parents' attitude. They even go so far as to say that prohibiting abuse is merely a new form of violence, that crimes should therefore not be designated as such so long as they are committed against one's own children. Otherwise parents would feel injured and end up taking their revenge on the child. This is the opinion voiced by almost all representatives of the medical world as well as of child protection agencies.

Nevertheless they are in error, and what speaks from their arguments is the fear of the once threatened child who would like to come to terms with his parents and is therefore prepared to remain silent and "not to notice." Reality does not bear them out. The Scandinavian countries have already entrenched in their laws a doctor's obligation to report child abuse, and, thanks to this legislation, the population has come to realize that the rights of children are not to be ignored. Moreover, my own experience has taught me that some parents react better to the truth than to soothing words and that they can benefit from correct information. Every human being caught in a trap will search for a way out. And at heart he is glad and grateful if he is shown a way out that does not lead to guilt or to the destruction of his own children. In most cases parents are not monsters who must be soothed with truisms to keep them from screaming;

often they are desperate children who must first learn to see reality and become aware of their responsibility. They could not learn this as children because their parents did not know of this responsibility; they misunderstood it as a right to abuse their power. Now it is up to the young parents to recognize those "precepts" as useless and to learn from their experience with their children. But this new process can take place only when it is clearly understood by the legislators, too, that child abuse damages a person for life and that this damage is in no way diminished by the ignorance of the perpetrator. It is only with the uncovering of the complete truth as it affects all those involved that a genuinely viable solution can be found to the dangers of child abuse.

Carl-Heinz Mallet's book *Untertan Kind* shows how, even since Martin Luther, pedagogues have exhorted parents to chastise and punish their children in God's place. Reading that book can help today's parents understand why they find themselves in an emotional trap and the price they and their children have to pay if they cling to the traditional values of childrearing. The inference may sound paradoxical, yet it is correct: The hitherto legal way out of the trap, the chastising of their child, leads to crime, and the hitherto prohibited way of "noticing," of criticizing their own parents, leads out of the state of guilt and to the salvation of our children. Mallet's book can be very helpful for parents who do not know my books and who will for the first time realize with horror what was once inflicted on them and what in their blindness they have been passing on. But it is through this horror that the door is beginning to open out of the compulsive destruction of life into freedom and responsibility.

NOTES

Preface

3 And we have statistics showing: *Newsletter of the American Psychological Association,* December 1983.

4 To demonstrate the hidden sources of violence: Miller, *For Your Own Good.*

5 Not to take one's own suffering seriously: These ideas are from a new, expanded version of part of the introduction to Miller, *The Drama of the Gifted Child,* 1986.

9 For when we no longer need to confront: Miller, *For Your Own Good,* pp. 281–84.

Part I

Chapter Two

29 but the completed cassette she sent me: Blair, *Children at Risk.*

33 "So what is a parent to do?": Donahue, *The Human Animal,* p. 211.

36 But in view of the great confusions they are causing: Miller, *The Untouched Key,* Part III, Chaps. 1, 2.

Chapter Three

38 In the American weekly *Newsday Magazine:* Jones, "Mothers Who Kill."

42 That which Martin Luther postulated: Mallet, *Untertan Kind.*

42 "Expressing these technical discoveries": Quoted by Montagu in *Growing Young,* p. 118.

42 "poisonous pedagogy": I define "poisonous pedagogy" in *Thou Shalt Not Be Aware* as "that tradition of childrearing which attempts to suppress all vitality, creativity, and feeling in the child and maintain the autocratic, godlike position of the parents at all costs" (p. 18). Also see my discussion of "poisonous pedagogy" in *For Your Own Good,* pp. 3–91.

42 Although the assertion of infantile sexuality: For a better understanding of what follows, see Miller, *Thou Shalt Not Be Aware,* pp. 107–59.

44 I demonstrated in *For Your Own Good:* pp. 198–243.

46 Erin Pizzey, the founder of shelters: *Scream Quietly or the Neighbors Will Hear.*

Chapter Four

54 The opinions most hotly defended: The evidence for the insights formulated in this chapter is to be found in my previous books; in particular, the reader will find my remarks about Freud easier to understand against the background of *Thou Shalt Not Be Aware,* Part III.

54 The dogmatizing of these false claims: See Miller, *The Untouched Key,* Part III, Chap. 2.

54 Freud originally discovered: Freud, "Zur Ätiologie der Hysterie."

55 A few months later: Freud, *Complete Letters,* pp. 264–66.

55 "Unfortunately, my own father": Freud, *Complete Letters,* pp. 230–31.

57 This perfect consensus with pedagogy: See Miller, *Thou Shalt Not Be Aware,* pp. 4n, 11–43.

58 Since the game of words: Ibid., pp. 252–56.

60 For, according to the American psychohistorian: de Mause, "Schreber and the History of Childhood."

65 "The estimated number of unreported cases": Trube-Becker, "Sexuelle Misshandlung von Kindern."

67 "It was my body's fault": From Allen, *Daddy's Girl,* quoted in Miller, *Thou Shalt Not Be Aware,* p. 320.

67 "Freud shrank from reality": Ibid., pp. 109ff

78 And as long as the child's feelings: Ibid., pp. 72–78.

80 By directing diffuse, nonspecific: See Miller, *The Untouched Key,* Part II.

Chapter Five

84 That it is not so was demonstrated: Leboyer, *Birth Without Violence.*

85 The inducing of labor: Armstrong and Feldman, *A Wise Birth.*

86 Rarely if ever are the mothers told: Miller, *The Drama of the Gifted Child,* pp. 47–84.

Chapter Six

100 "In her personality my mother remained constant": Kügelgen, *Jugenderinnerungen eines alten Mannes.* Excerpt translated by Leila Vennewitz.

101 "My excellent father was": Schopenhauer, *Ein Lebensbild in Briefen.* Excerpt translated by Leila Vennewitz.

102 "It is my desire that you learn": Ibid. Excerpt translated by Leila Vennewitz.

105 "TYRONE (*Goaded into vindictiveness.*)": O'Neill, *Long Day's Journey into Night,* pp. 142–54.

116 "For Carlotta": Ibid., p. 7.

118 "That was in the winter of senior year": Ibid., p. 176.

119 "EDMUND . . . Listen, Mama": Ibid., pp. 119–21.

Chapter Seven

135 "For thousands of years": Morris, *Bodywatching,* pp. 218–20.

NOTES

Part II

Chapter One

156 What this father had learned as a child: See Miller, *The Untouched Key*, Part III, Chap. 1.

159 And the analysts were convinced: See Miller, *Thou Shalt Not Be Aware*, pp. 37–43.

159 Although their explanations were derived: See Miller, *The Untouched Key*, Part III, Chap. 2.

Chapter Two

167 "I have read your three books": Personal correspondence, 1986.

170 he also discovered, many decades ago: Montagu, *Touching*.

174 But we are moving in the right direction: See Miller, *The Untouched Key*, Part III, Chap. 2.

175 Daniel's history, told in the next chapter: See also ibid., Part III, Chaps. 1, 2.

Chapter Three

177 "I once took my three-year-old Daniel": Personal correspondence, 1985.

Chapter Four

183 For the analyst to be able to do this: See Miller, *Thou Shalt Not Be Aware*, pp. 252–56.

183 The patient senses that inability: See Miller, *The Drama of the Gifted Child*, pp. 39ff.

186 Until a few years ago: See Miller, *The Untouched Key*, Part II.

188 And they do not see through the abuse: See Miller, *Thou Shalt Not Be Aware*, pp. 17–23.

188 The man who was no longer allowed: Miller, *The Untouched Key*, Part III, Chap. 2.

BIBLIOGRAPHY

ALLEN, CHARLOTTE VALE. *Daddy's Girl.* Toronto: McLelland & Stewart, 1980.

ARMSTRONG, PENNY, and SHERYL FELDMAN. *A Wise Birth.* New York: William Morrow, 1990.

BLAIR, WENDY. *Children at Risk: For the Love of Children.* National Public Radio, Washington, D.C., 1985.

CLARAC, VIVIANE. *De la honte à la colère* (From Shame to Anger). Paris: Les Publications Anonymes, 1985.

DE MAUSE, LLOYD. "Schreber and the History of Childhood." Unpublished manuscript, 1987.

DONAHUE, PHIL. *The Human Animal.* New York: Simon & Schuster, 1985.

FLIESS, ROBERT. *Symbol, Dream, and Psychosis.* New York: International University Press, 1973.

BIBLIOGRAPHY

FREUD, SIGMUND. "Zur Ätiologie der Hysterie" (On the Etiology of Hysteria). In *Studienausgabe,* vol. 6. Frankfurt: Fischer, 1886.

————. *The Complete Letters of Sigmund Freud to Wilhelm Fliess, 1887–1904.* Translated and edited by Jeffrey Masson. Cambridge: Harvard University Press, 1985.

GLOVER, EDWARD. *The Roots of Crime.* New York: International University Press. Quoted by Montagu in *Growing Young.*

JANOV, ARTHUR. *The Primal Scream.* New York: Putnam's, 1970.

JONES, ANN. "Mothers Who Kill." *Newsday Magazine,* 19 October 1986.

KÜGELGEN, WILHELM V. *Jugenderinnerungen eines alten Mannes* (Youthful Memories of an Old Man). Zurich: Manesse, 1970.

LEBOYER, FREDERICK. *Birth Without Violence.* New York: Knopf, 1975.

MALLET, CARL-HEINZ. *Untertan Kind* (The Subject Child). Munich: Hueber, 1987.

MEHR, MARIELLA. *Steinzeit* (Stone Age). Bern: Zytglogge, 1986.

MILLER, ALICE. *Prisoners of Childhood.* Translated by Ruth Ward. New York: Basic Books, 1981. Reissued in paperback as *The Drama of the Gifted Child.* Basic Books, 1982.

————. *For Your Own Good: Hidden Cruelty in Child-Rearing and the Roots of Violence.* Translated by Hildegarde and Hunter Hannum. New York: Farrar, Straus, and Giroux, 1983.

————. *Thou Shalt Not Be Aware: Society's Betrayal of the Child.* Translated by Hildegarde and Hunter Hannum. New York: New American Library, 1984.

————. *Pictures of a Childhood.* Translated by Hildegarde and Hunter Hannum. New York: Farrar, Straus, and Giroux, 1986.

————. *The Untouched Key: Tracing Childhood Trauma in Creativity and Destructiveness.* Translated by Hildegarde and Hunter Hannum. New York: Doubleday, 1990.

MILLER, ARTHUR. *Death of a Salesman.* New York: Viking, 1945.

MONTAGU, ASHLEY. *Growing Young.* New York: McGraw-Hill, 1981.

————. *Touching: The Human Significance of the Skin.* New York: Harper & Row, 1986.

MORRIS, DESMOND. *Bodywatching.* London: Jonathan Cape, 1985.

O'NEILL, EUGENE. *Long Day's Journey into Night.* New Haven: Yale University Press, 1956.

PIZZEY, ERIN. *Scream Quietly or the Neighbors Will Hear.* Hillside, N.J.: Enslow, 1979 (pbk.).

BIBLIOGRAPHY

Psychologie heute: Wie Therapien das Kind verraten (Psychology Today: How Therapies Betray the Child). April 1987.

SCHOPENHAUER, ARTHUR. *Ein Lebensbild in Briefen* (Picture of a Life in Letters). Edited by Angelika Hübscher. Frankfurt: Insel, 1987.

STETTBACHER, J. KONRAD. *Wenn Leiden einen Sinn haben soll* (If Suffering Is to Have a Meaning). Hamburg: Hoffmann & Campe, 1990.

TRUBE-BECKER, ELISABETH. "Sexuelle Misshandlung von Kindern: Soziologische Gesichtspunkte" (Sexual Abuse of Children: Sociological Aspects). In *Das öffentliche Gesundheitswesen* (Public Health), no. 5, May 1987.

INDEX

206